ADAM TO ABRAHAM

The Early History of Man

*Pamela,
I hope you find this book enlightening.*

by

Thomas Coley Allen

Thomas Coley Allen

TC Allen Company

Copyright © 1998 by
Thomas Coley Allen
All rights reserved

Published by
TC Allen Company
13 Garner Road
Franklinton, North Carolinas 27525

Library of Congress Catalog Number: 98-92753

ISBN: 0-9656663-1-X

Printed in the United States of America by
Morris Publishing
3212 East Highway 30
Kearney, Nebraska 68847
1-800-650-7888

CONTENTS

Preface 1

1 Overview 4
    The Adamic Race 5
    Scripture and Science 6
    Creation 12
    The Flood 13
    Evolution 14

2 Creation of the Universe and Earth 16
    Creation of Universe 16
    Creation of the Earth 18
    The Six-Day Creation Theory 20
    Other Creation Theories 24
    The Day-Age Theory 26
    Six Days of Creation 30
    Why Describe Creation as Occurring
        In Six Days? 38

3 Creation of Man 40
    Monogenesis or Polygenesis 41
    Pre-Adamic Men 51
    Creation of Adam 58
    What Race Was Adam? 66
    Image of God 69
    Location of Eden 71
    The Serpent in the Garden of Eden 75

When Did the Fall Occur? 77

4 From the Fall to the Flood 78
   Did Death Occur Before Adam Sinned? 78
   Where Did Adam Go When Driven from Eden? . 83
   Rise of the Cainites 84
   Pre-Flood Migration of Aryans 87

5 The Flood 94
   Use of the Word "All" 94
   Use of the Word "Earth" 95
   Races of Men Support a Local Flood 96
   Animal Life Supports a Local Flood 101
   Plant Life Support to a Local Flood 106
   The Rainbow Covenant Supports
      a Local Flood 109
   Geology Supports a Local Flood 109
   Geography Supports a Local Flood 115
   Civilization after the Flood Supports
      a Local Flood 116
   Diverseness of Flood Stories Supports
      a Local Flood 122
   Jesus' Comments Supports a Local Flood 125
   Where Did the Flood Occur? 129
   The Rainbow 131
   Why Did God Send the Flood 133
   Purpose of the Ark 135

6 Following the Flood 137
   The Descendants of Noah 138
   The Japhethites 139
   The Hamites 141
   Curse of Canaan 143
   The Shemites 144

       Nimrod 145
       Post-Flood Migration of Aryans 147
       Abraham 152

7 Astral Catastrophism 154
       Tower of Babel Catastrophe 155
       Peleg Catastrophe 156
       The Flood Catastrophe 156
       Enosh Catastrophe 157
       Pre-Adamic Catastrophe 157
       Canopy Theory 157

8 Conclusion 161

Appendices 165
       Appendix 1. Chronology 165
       Appendix 2. Tarim Basin 178
       Appendix 3. Early Man and the Stone Age . . . 180
       Appendix 4. The Species of Men 182
       Appendix 5. Early Rulers of Egypt 183
       Appendix 6. Ancient Peoples of Palestine 185
       Appendix 7. Laws of Nature 190
       Appendix 8. Law of Faunal Succession 191
       Appendix 9. Adam's First Wife 192
       Appendix 10. Geocentric Universe 193
       Appendix 11. Create 197
       Appendix 12. Man: 'Âdâm and Îysh 198

References 201

Index 215
       Subject Index 215
       Scripture Index 231

PREFACE

This book is aimed primarily at the Christian who instinctively knows that a common origin of all races of men is impossible. Yet they have been taught through dated misinterpretations of the Bible that all mankind descended from Adam through Noah. When they look at the races of men, they wonder how can this be. This book resolves that conflict. It shows that not all races of men descended from Adam or Noah. Only the White or Aryan race descended from them.

Liberal theology is rarely mentioned in the following pages. Like the rest of the liberal establishment, their hatred of the White race and their desire for its demise is obvious. The conservative racialist Christian is aware of the liberal's attacks and can deflect them.

The White Christian's real threat comes from misguided conservative theologians, which also includes theologians who are called orthodox and fundamentalists. Therefore, most of the discussion that follows concerns conservative and traditional theology. Although not all these theologians may hate the White race, their adherence to dated misinterpretation of the Scriptures results in the same end, the demise of the White race. By erroneously claiming all mankind descended from Adam through Noah, they destroy the greatest barrier to integration and resulting miscegenation, which explains why most of them are integrationists. By proclaiming that races descended from Adam through Noah and that the

Flood was universal, they become evolutionists although they vigorously deny it. As far as the death of the White race is concerned, nothing much distinguishes them from the liberal theologians. They are, however, much more dangerous because their attacks are covert, indirect, and unobvious.

Nearly all liberal preachers and far too many conservative preachers have taught White Christians that they must sacrifice themselves to the other races of men in the name of brotherly love. Their doctrine of brotherly love demands the hatred of the White race. The White race must destroy itself for the sake of equality and unity of mankind. Their doctrine of equality, unity of man, and brotherly love have supplanted the true teaching of the Bible. The Bible clearly teaches racial separation, preservation of racial integrity, and inequality of man. These doctrines the false teachers despise most.

Not too long ago nearly all these false teachers were liberal theologians. Today nearly all conservative theologians are also false teachers. As far as their doctrines on race, equality, and the unity of man are concerned, no differences remain between them and the liberals. The liberals have won. They have converted the conservatives. Conservatives have abandoned the teachings of the Bible on race and have adopted the teachings of liberals.

Conservatives base their false teachings on false interpretations of the Bible. They claim that all the races of men descended from Adam. They are wrong. As this book clearly shows, only the White race (or more correctly, species) descended from Adam. Conservatives claim that the races of men descended from Noah because a universal flood killed everyone except Noah and his family. Again they are wrong. Only part of the White race descended from Noah (therefore, the Flood was not universal). The following pages expose these and other errors of these false teachers.

In writing this book, the author hopes to remove the suicidal guilt that far too many Christian Whites seem to possess. It supports what many people intuitively know is true: The primary races of men are species of different origins. Further, they also intuitively know that science is closer to the truth about the age of the Earth, the age of men, and the lack of a universal flood a few thousand years ago than the claims of conservatives. Finally, these people intuitively know that the major error of science today is biological evolution. Because biological evolution is false, they know that the claims of conservatives are wrong because these claims are built on the foundation of evolution.

May Aryans free themselves from the chains of self-hatred that bind them so that they can glorify and serve their Creator and His Son. Faith is not believing what one knows is false; faith is believing what one knows is true. May the truth set them free.

1
OVERVIEW

This book gives a general brief overview of the early history of the Aryan* race (or more correctly, the Aryan

---

*"Aryan" is used for the White race for several reasons. First, it is perhaps the most politically incorrect term to use. Second, the more common term "Caucasian" generally includes many people, such as the inhabitants of India, who do not properly belong to the White race. (They are part of the Melanochroic species.) "European" suffers a similar problem and is even more misleading and confusing when used to refer to people of the Middle East and northern Africa. Many may object to the use of "Aryan" because it describes a language group (Indo-European) and not a race. (Though only a few will admit it, most really object to the use of "Aryan" because Hitler and his followers corrupted the use of the word as an excuse for conquest.) This objection is irrational because language names are commonly used as racial names. Examples are Celt, Semitic, Berber, Tungus, Chinese, Turk, Mongolian, Malay, Polynesian, Lapp, Eskimo, Bantu, Hamite, Arab, Khoisan, and Melanesian. "Aryan" was commonly used in the nineteenth and into the early twentieth century as a racial name. Further, the word rolls off the tongue better than other names for this race or species. For these reasons, among others, is why "Aryan" is used although the primary reason is to prevent confusion with what "Caucasian" has come to represent.

species of men),* which involves bridging the chasm between Scripture and science.

Without questions the author accepts the Bible as the truth, the Divine revelation of God to man. The Bible should not be, and does not need to be, proved from science. Science is merely a tool to help man better to understand God's work, His creation. When both science and the Bible are properly understood, any need to misinterpret facts or twist the truth to obtain agreement between science and the Scriptures no longer remains. Nature reveals God's presence and His creative powers through His work. True science is merely a description of God's work. The Bible is God's verbal revelation of Himself to man and informs man verbally of his duty to God. Nature and Scriptures are a unity. They have the same author. When properly understood, they harmonize without contradiction or inconsistency.

The Adamic Race

The Bible is the story of the White or Aryan race.† "This is the book of the generations of Adam. In the day that God created man [Adam], in the likeness of God made he him; male and female created him them, and blessed them, and called their name Adam, in the day

---

*When referring to man, species and race are used synonymously throughout this book. That is, the primary races of men are species of men.

†Adamite, White, and Aryan are used synonymously throughout this book.

when they were created."* (Genesis 5:1,2) It begins with the Aryan race in general and narrows to one nation—Israel; then it narrows to one person—Jesus, who is the climax and purpose of the Bible and the Aryan race—nay all mankind. It does not contain the genesis of the other races of man; science has to be consulted for their genesis. The Bible only traces the Aryan race back to Adam.

Scripture and Science

This book, in part, attempts to bridge the chasm that exists between the findings of science and the traditional interpretation of the first eleven chapters of Genesis. Science, God's work, should be interpreted in light of the Scriptures, and the Scriptures, God's word, should be interpreted in the light of science. There is no conflict or contradiction between science and the Scriptures. Because God is the author of both nature and the Scriptures, no conflict or contradiction can exist between the two. Where conflicts or contradictions appear to exist, they result from man's lack of understanding of science or the Scriptures or both.†

Science has its limitations. Diversions it can bring, but true joy it cannot bring. The Universe it can analyze,

---

*Biblical quotations are from the American Standard Version, 1901, unless otherwise noted.

†This is true of the Scriptures themselves. Since the Bible contains no conflicts or contradictions, what may appear to be a conflict or contradiction in the Bible results from man's lack of understanding.

but a quark* it cannot create. Death to millions it can bring, but the dead it cannot resurrect. Although it can speculate, science cannot with certainty tell man his origin, his destiny, or his reason for being. Science fails to offer man the highest means for expression. To forgive sin, to wipe away all record of sin, and to save a soul, science is of no value at all. It cannot regenerate, redeem, or sanctify. The realm of science is strictly limited to analyzing the physical world. It is a tool, one of many tools, for man to use to understand the Universe. Although science can explain how man does interact with God and his fellow man, it cannot explain how man should interact. In the realm of the Divine, salvation, ethics, and morality, science is a severely limited tool.

On the other hand, the Bible provides man information that science cannot provide. It provides man the most important information that he can possess. God's revelations are given to man through His word, the Bible. It reveals the character of God to man.

The Bible is, without question, the truth, the Divine revelation of God to man. Because the Bible, including Genesis, is God's revelation, its record of creation is a trustworthy historical account. It should not be, and does not need to be, proved from science. Science is merely a tool to help man to understand better God's work, His creation. When both science and the Bible are properly understood, no need remains to misinterpret facts or twist the truth to obtain agreement between science and the Scriptures.

---

*Quarks are particles of which protons are made.

Both science and Scriptures testify to the orderliness of the Universe. The Scriptures declare, "While the earth remaineth, seedtime and harvest, and cold and heat, and summer and winter, and day and night shall not cease" (Genesis 8:22). "For everything there is a season, and a time for every purpose under heaven" (Ecclesiastics 3:1). "The wind goeth toward the south, and turneth about unto the north; it turneth about continually in its course, and the wind returneth again to its circuits. All the rivers run into the sea, yet the sea is not full; unto the place whither the rivers go, thither they go again" (Ecclesiastes 1:6-7). "God is not a God of confusion, but of peace" (1 Corinthians 14:33a). Science confirms these Scriptural observations. (Or, more accurately, these passages confirm the discoveries of science.)*

Too many people fail to differentiate interpretation from inspiration. Revelation is not interpretation, and interpretation is not revelation. God communicates Divine truth by revelation. Man's efforts to understand His revelation is by interpretation.

The purpose of the first chapter of Genesis is religion, not science. God wrote the scientific account of creation on the crust of the Earth and in the heavens. The religious account of creation is written in the first chapter of Genesis. Both accounts are from God and should be understood as such and received accordingly.

In interpreting Genesis, identifying a given world view with its science with the Bible should be avoided.

---

*God has so blessed man with the orderliness of His Universe and with the dependability of His natural laws that man can act and achieve a known outcome without knowing the laws of nature involved.

Deriving too much specific data from the generalities of Genesis should also be avoided. Scientific data, knowledge, and records change with time. What was considered an excellent hypothesis yesterday may be proven false tomorrow.

Furthermore, in understanding Genesis, one must realize that the Bible is not written in scientific language. It is written in the vernacular. The language is also phenomenal, i.e., it discusses things the way the senses perceive them. The Bible describes things in common everyday language and the way things appear, not necessarily the way they are. For example, it describes the solar system as geocentric instead of heliocentric. As people still do today, it describes the Sun as rising and setting instead of the Earth rotating. The Bible describes natural things, but it does not explain them. It records observations of nature without any theoretical explanation of the natural thing observed.

Data acquired from the study of nature should lead to, or suggest, reevaluating the data of the Bible to see if they have been interpreted correctly the first time. Nature, however, should not be used to force interpretation on the Bible. The Bible must finally be interpreted in terms of itself. Literature, archaeology, geology, astronomy, and other sources of information may be used to ask the proper questions of the Biblical text to arrive at the proper interpretation. For example, the Biblical text of the Scripture and Biblical analogy must determine the interpretation of the length of days in Genesis One. Information from nature should not decide it. Information from nature should merely agree with and support the interpretation.

An example of science causing reevaluation of Scriptural interpretation is the work of Copernicus and Galileo. The Church interpreted the Scriptures to mean that the world was flat and at the center of the solar system and Universe.* Astronomy and physics proved that the globe was spherical, which the ancient Greeks knew, and that it revolved around the Sun. After much persecution and denying the facts, the Church finally reevaluated its interpretation of the Scriptures and concluded that a spherical Earth revolving around the Sun did not conflict with the Scriptures. It had misunderstood the Scriptures.

For those who claim that science is being used to interpret the Scriptures and that the Scriptures are being forced to conform with currently held scientific concepts, i.e., the Scriptures are being subordinated to science, they need to remember that the Church once held that the Scriptures required a geocentric solar system and Universe. Science showed that the solar system was heliocentric. Now no clergyman seriously considers the Earth to be the center of the solar system. Likewise, the Church once believed that all the stars revolved around the Earth every 24 hours. Science proved otherwise.† The Scriptures had merely described the Universe from an Earth perspective.

---

*See Appendix 10 for Scriptural arguments supporting the theory of the Earth as the center of the Universe.

†The great reformer Martin Luther in his Commentary on the Book of Genesis claimed that both the stars and planets derived their light from the Sun and that the Sun and all the other heavenly bodies move around the earth in 24 hours.

The fossil record offers a similar example. When people first began seriously studying fossils, the Church, for the most part, held that fossils were not the remains of living creatures. God had created fossils and placed them in rocks to tempt man's faith, or alternatively, the devil made them to destroy man's faith.* Such an interpretation had to be true based on the then current interpretation and understanding of the Scriptures. Yet today few clergymen would seriously claim that fossils are not the remains of once living creatures.

Many scientific advances have met the cries of heresy, work of the devil, and "if this is true, the Bible is a lie"—Christianity would soon die. Among such heresies and deathblows to the Bible and Christianity have been the existence of antipodes. If antipodes existed, then the Bible, which in many places describes the Earth as a plane with four corners, etc., was false; Christ was a hoax; and the Church was dead. Surgical operations were mutilation and a wicked attempt to evade the curse of the Fall. Anaesthesia and painkillers were sinful means to avoid

---

*Several hypotheses were proposed to explain the presence of fossils. One was when God commanded the Earth to bring forth life, some life forms became stuck in the rocks and were unable to make the journey out of the earth. They were fossilized. Another hypothesis was that fossils resulted from the plastic power of nature. A third held that they were products of fatty matter set into fermentation by heat. Others hypothesized that the fossils were products of lapidific fluid or the seminal air. Some claimed that they resulted from sports of nature or a tumultuous movement of terrestrial exaltations. Many Christians believed that the fossils were a result of the Flood. This view is still popular today.

the curse of the Fall. Lightening rods were insults to God. Closing open sewers interfered with God's use of plagues to punish sin. How many of today's Christians are guilty of one or more of these heresies? Has Christianity been damaged by any of these scientific advances? No clergyman today considers all these heresies. Rare is a clergyman who would consider any of them a heresy.

Have the scientific discoveries that led to a change in Biblical interpretation resulted in subordinating the Scriptures to science. No! They have lead to a better understanding of the Scriptures. So it is with the creation of the Universe and all therein and the Flood.

The truth and data of the Scriptures exist independently of the theories and opinions of science. The Scriptures are infallible while science is not. Science changes with time while the Scriptures remain constant.*

Creation

The Six-Day Creation Theory and the Restitution Theory are invalid interpretation of Genesis and are, therefore, rejected. The Six-Day Creation Theory claims that the Universe, Earth, and all life-forms were created between 12,000 and 6,000 years ago in six literal 24-hour days. According to the Restitution Theory, Genesis 1:1 describes the creation of the Universe and Earth and Genesis 1:3 and following describe six literal 24-hour days of creative activity that occurred between 6,000 and

---

*The claim that the races of men have a common ancestor is current scientific dogma, a dogma that most conservative, liberal and fundamental clergymen have adopted. This dogma, however, lacks the support of the Scriptures and science.

12,000 years ago. Hundreds of millions of years may have elapsed between Genesis 1:1 and Genesis 1:3. Granted, both, and especially the first theory, can be proven by a strict literal reading of the first chapter of Genesis and can be supported by a strict literal reading of other select verses. That the Earth is the center of the Universe and that the Sun, planets, and stars rotate around the Earth can also be proven by a strict literal reading of the Bible. The interpretation that the Earth is the center of the Universe with the Sun, planets and stars rotating around it has been rejected because the observable facts do not support this interpretation. Likewise, the various other theories that hold that creation occurred within 144 consecutive hours are rejected because the observable facts do not support them.

The first impression of reading Genesis One is that the days are literal 24-hour days. The first impression of reading some passages of the Bible is not always the correct one. After reflection and further study of the Scriptures, the first impression may be reevaluated, and a different interpretation adopted. Furthermore, Genesis One can be read and interpreted in a way that removes the conflict with most observable scientific facts* without doing violence to the Scriptures.

The Flood

The universal flood theory is rejected. Although much geological evidence can be used to support the universal flood theory, much geological evidence can also

---

*Where conflict continues to exist, it is due to a lack of information.

be used to disprove this theory. One major problem with the universal flood theory is that evolution must be accepted to support it. This is especially true of the Whitcomb and Morris theory, which is one of the most popular theories of the universalists. It is also true of the astral catastrophe theory of Patten.* Furthermore, the Scriptures can be read and interpreted just as easily to support a great local flood as they can to support a universal flood. The local flood interpretation does not do violence to the Bible and over all is more compatible with it.

Evolution

Biological or organic evolution is rejected: be it secular evolution or theistic evolution; be it evolution over many generations and thousands of millions of years or over a few generations and tens of decades. The transmutation of species is denied.

Principal Dawson sums up the flaws of evolution,
The evolutionist doctrine is one of the strangest phenomena of humanity. It existed, and most naturally, in the oldest philosophy and poetry, in connection with the crudest and most uncritical attempts of the human mind to grasp the system

---

*The authors and supporters of these theories claim to reject evolution. While denying evolution, they resort to evolution in maintaining their theories of a universal flood several millennia ago. What they deny is the evolutionary theory of the secular and theorist evolutionists where one species gradually changes into another species over thousands of generations. Their theory of evolution requires one species to evolve into another species within a few generations.

of nature; but that in our day a system destitute of any shadow of proof, and supported merely by vague analysis and figures of speech, and by the arbitrary and artificial coherence of its own parts, should be accepted as philosophy, and should find able adherents to string on its thread of hypotheses our vast and weighty stores of knowledge, is surprisingly strange.*

As is shown throughout this book, the traditional creationist theory is evolution disguised. Traditional creationists claim that all the species of men descended from Adam through Noah. In short they claim that like beget unlike—hence, evolution. A false dichotomy is offered by the traditional creationists and conservative theologians on one hand and the theistic evolutionists and liberal theologians on the other hand with their misinterpretations of the Bible. At least the theistic evolutionists and liberal theologians are more honest, for they do not conceal their support of evolution.

If the traditional creationist rejects what is presented in this book, he must prove his theory true without having to resort to a disguised form of evolution. So far he has failed to do so. His theory ultimately depends on evolution. It conflicts with science and is not always consistent with the Scriptures. This book does present a theory that is consistent with both science and Scripture and that does not have to resort to any kind of evolution.

---

*[William H. Campbell], *Anthropology for the People: A Refutation of the Theory of the Adamic Origin of All Races* (Richmond, 1891), p. 87.

2
CREATION OF THE UNIVERSE AND EARTH

Science claims that the Universe has existed for about 15 billion years. Using Biblical chronology, the Bible student finds the Universe being created about six thousand or seventy-five hundred years ago. Who is right?

Creation of Universe

Genesis 1:1 reads, "In the beginning God created the heaven and the earth." When did the beginning occur? The Bible does not say. The Bible identifies who created the Universe, not when it was created. It could have been 6,000 or 6,000,000,000 years ago. Science indicates that the age of the earth is closer to the latter than the former.*

According to Genesis 1:1, the Universe is finite. It has a definite beginning. Science agrees that the Universe has

---

*There are disagreements over the various methodologies used to measure the age of the earth. Each of these methods have problems, flaws, and uncertainties. Science cannot with a great deal of accuracy date the age of the Earth. However, the scientific evidence dates the creation of the Earth way before 4,000 B.C.

a beginning. According to best measures of science, the age of the Universe is about 15 billion years old.

Science and the Scriptures are in general agreement as to the beginning of the Universe. Both hold that it began out of nothing. Both claim that the Universe came into being suddenly and instantaneously. According to the "Big Bang" theory on the origin of the universe, there was nothing in the beginning. No energy, matter, space, time, or Universe existed. Here is where science stops or should stop. It cannot legitimately go beyond this point. Beyond this point is the realm of philosophy and religion. Beyond this point man must depend on revelation. God's revealed word in the Scriptures informs man about the origin of the Universe. According to the Bible, out of this nothing, God created the universe. Its mass, energy, time, and space came into being out of the will of God. God spoke, and it was (Psalm 33:6 and Hebrews 11:3).* God willed the Universe and all therein into existence. He brought the Universe and all that is in it into being in six successive stages in a definite order. If He so desired, He could will it and every inhabitant thereof, past and present, out of existence except those whom His Son has saved.

Genesis 1:1 refers primarily to the formation of the primitive material from which the more organized Universe was developed. A totally new structure, the Universe, had come into existence. It did not come into

---

*"By the word of Jehovah were heavens made, And all the host of them by the breath of his mouth." (Psalm 33:6) ". . . the world came into being by the command of God, so that what is seen does not owe its existence to that which is visible." (Hebrews 11:3)—Weymouth.

existence spontaneously or gradually through any agency other than God. God willed the Universe into existence Himself. One "moment" no Universe existed. The next moment, Bang! Time, space, energy, and matter, i.e., the Universe came into being. As with any new structure, the Universe could not have evolved or developed spontaneously. It came into existence by an act of God, which was purely miraculous. Only the initial material from which the fully organized Universe developed needed to be formed miraculously. This much must have been miraculous. The creation of the stars, planets, and other elements of the Universe did not require any miraculous events after the initial miraculous event. This is not to say that miraculous events did not later occur.

Creation of the Earth

Both science and Scripture are in general agreement on the formation of the Earth. Genesis 1:2* describes the beginning of the Earth as "waste and void" or "without form and empty."

Science describes the Earth as formed from hot gases collapsing into a dense gaseous ball that cooled and condensed further into molten metals and rocks. This molten ball of metal and rock cooled and condensed until the crest was formed. After further cooling and

---

*The second verse of Genesis is not a continuation of the narrative of the first verse. It is describing the beginning of something new. The first verse concerns the creation of the material out of which the Earth would be made. The second verse describes the actual formation of the Earth itself.

condensing, the Earth began to take shape as it is known today. Hence, the Earth began as waste and void.*

The Hebrew words used in the phrase "waste and void" are *tôhûw* (Strongs O. T. #8414) and *bôhûw* (Strongs O. T. #922). They have the same meaning, which is "empty space, without form, nothing, void, desolate." Thus, science and Scripture are in general agreement on the condition of the Earth when it was first formed. Both agree that the Earth in its early formation was not habitable. Hence, it was desolate.

The primary disagreement between science and traditional Christian interpretations of the Scriptures is primarily about when the creation of the Universe and Earth took place. Science generally places the creation of the Universe about 15 billion years ago and the formation of the Earth about 4.5 billion years ago. Although traditional Christian interpreters disagree about when the Universe and Earth were created, many place their creation no earlier than 10,000 years ago. To harmonize scientific estimations with the Scriptures, some interpreters place billions of years between verses one and two and verse three.

---

*When God initially formed the Earth, it was "without form and void." It was a mass of matter. God did not intend for the Earth to remain in such condition: "For thus saith Jehovah that created the heavens, the God that formed the earth and made it, that established it and created it not waste [or, in vain], that formed it to be inhabited. . . ." (Isaiah 45:18).

The Six-Day Creation Theory

The traditional interpretation of the first chapter of Genesis is that the six days described therein are six ordinary 24-hour days. All creation occurred in 144 hours.*

This interpretation as presented by Whitcomb and Morris holds that nearly all pre-fossil sedimentary rock was formed during these six days.† (The fossil bearing sedimentary rock was formed during the Flood although some contend that the fossil record of plants may have started on the third day.) According to their theory, most likely only one major continent existed before the Noahic Flood. (However, the number of continents is not

---

*The irony of a strictly literal interpretation of Genesis One by conservative theologians is that it allies them with liberal theologians. Liberal theologians insist on a strict interpretation to discredit and mythicize Genesis One. The conservatives do it to enhance the power and sovereignty of God. Both reduce the ancient Hebrews to ignorant buffoons by insisting on a strict literal interpretation.

†Most six-day creationists seem to confuse geology with biology. They believe that if the Earth is more than about 20,000 years old, evolution is proved. They fail to realize that geology is independent of biology. True, geologists use fossils to aid in dating rock strata. However, whether these organisms were created or evolved is immaterial to the geological dating scheme. The date remains the same regardless of how the fossilized creatures came into being. Secular evolution does require an old Earth; but as is repeatedly shown throughout this book, evolution does not necessarily require an old Earth. The Six-Day Creation Theory when coupled with the universal flood theory demands rapid evolution.

essential to this theory.) A thick canopy of water vapor lay above the troposphere. This canopy maintained a relatively constant temperature around the globe; little wind and no rain occurred. The six days of creation occurred recently—no more than about 10,000 to 15,000 years ago.* The Universe and Earth were created with apparent age, i.e., they were created to appear billions of years old.† (Hence, supporters of this theory are often called mature creationists.) Proof that the Earth was created old is that soil necessary to sustain plant life could not be formed within a few hours. It must have been formed with apparent age.

Furthermore, the laws of nature that exist today did not exist during the six days of creation.# Six-day

---

*The idea that the Earth is very young is based on a very rigid interpretation of a few verses. Nowhere does the Bible specifically state that the Earth is only a few thousand years old.

†Once one claims that the Earth was created with apparent age, he can no longer tell what really happened in the past from what only appears to have happened. He does not know for sure if the Universe was created six billion years, six million years, six thousand years, or six years ago. To assign a time becomes completely arbitrary. The Universe could have been created six minutes ago, and all that one believes to be history and past experiences is merely apparent age.

#By denying natural processes in creation, the six-day creationists seem to believe that the forces of nature are not of God. Jesus spoke otherwise. He said, "he [God] maketh his sun to rise on the evil and the good, and sendeth rain on the just and the unjust." (Matthew 5:45b) Jesus and the writers of the

creationists claim that the laws of nature before Adam's fall differed from those laws that existed after his fall. In other words, God's seventh day of rest ended, and He began His eighth day of work by creating a new set of physical and biological laws. (Such a concept is alien to the Bible. The Bible does not discuss an eighth day of work. To the contrary the Bible shows that God's rest continues to this day.)

To the six-day creationists, the events that occurred during the creation week are essentially a series of instantaneous, miraculous Divine acts involving virtually no natural processes. These events consist in the formation of totally new structure rather than the shaping or forming of preexistent material. Creation was a series of instantaneous acts of producing new things out of nothing. Six-day creationists fear that if all the six days of creation are not completely miraculous Divine acts totally free of all natural processes, then the sovereignty of God is impugned and assaulted.*

Scriptures saw all natural processes as the work of God. God is not divorced from natural processes. To the contrary He uses them to execute His will. That is why He created them. Being transcendent, He can act outside of nature and natural process. Being immanent, He can also act through nature and natural processes. Any interpretation that excludes all natural causes is as out of harmony with the Scriptures as is one that excludes all Divine action.

*To claim that the processes that exist today existed during the time of creation does not constitute an attack on the sovereignty of God. God created these processes. The Bible reveals the sovereignty of God in history, in day-to-day affairs of man and nature, and even in the ordinary process of rising

Six-day creationists claim that the second law of thermodynamics* could not have existed before the fall. This is not true. It could and probably has existed in this Universe since its creation. The expenditure of energy can overcome the second law at a particular place for a particular time. If this were not true, the internal combustion engine could not work. The second law of thermodynamics does prove that the Universe had a definite beginning in time. If the Universe were infinitely old, every point in the Universe would have the same temperature.

Among the many things that six-day creationists have in common with the evolutionists is that both hold theories that make scientific study of the past fruitless. The six-day creationists hold that the laws of nature changed with Adam's fall. (Some who are universalists also seem to hold that other changes occurred with the Flood.) They claim that Divine fiat without any natural processes or laws influencing the material being formed

---

and setting of the Sun. Natural processes are going on today, and God is as sovereign as He was during the creation week. The real issue is not the sovereignty of God. The issue is whether or not the creation week of the Bible is totally devoid of any thought of natural process.

*The second law of thermodynamics asserts that the entropy of a system or process cannot decrease; it must remain constant or increase. Entropy is a measure of the extent to which the energy of a system is unavailable; the higher the entropy the less energy available. According to the second law of thermodynamics, all energy eventually ends up in an unusable form.

or created caused the events that occurred during the six days of creation. Laws of nature did not come into existence until the completion of creation. Some evolutionists in an attempt to eliminate God completely claim that the laws of nature evolved as the Universe evolved. Thus, the laws of nature that man has discovered in recent millennia may be entirely different from those billions of years ago. If either is true, then science is useless in exploring the formation of anything during the creation era.*

Other Creation Theories

Several other interpretative theories have been developed in an attempt to harmonize science with the Scriptures. These include the Framework Theory, Restitution Theory, and the Day Age Theory.†

According to the Framework Theory, the days of Genesis One are not regarded chronologically. They are understood symbolically like the numbered sequences of the visions in the Book of Revelation. They are not to be understood as so many periods, either shorter or longer.

---

*A more in depth discussion of the Six-Day Creation Theory is found in *The Genesis Flood* by John Whitcomb and Henry Morris (pro) and *Christianity & the Age of the Earth* by Davis Young (con).

†There is also the strictly spiritual interpretation theory, which Ryle advocates. Genesis One should not be viewed as revealing anything about science. It should be read strictly from the point of view of spiritual revelation. Thus, no attempt should be or needs to be made to reconcile science and Scripture.

A variant of this theory is the Pictorial Day Theory, which claims that creation was not performed in six days but was revealed in six days.*

According to the Restitution Theory, an immense indeterminate amount of time elapses in Genesis 1:1 and 2 before the six days of creation begin in verse three. This long period is sufficient to account for the needs of geology and astronomy. A variant of this theory holds that the immense indeterminate amount of time occurs with verse one. The condition of the Earth described in verse two is a relatively recent event. The Earth *became* waste and void, not *was* waste and void. God then adjusted the Earth to its presently existing condition over a six 24-hour day period. Another variant of this theory, which Joe Pye Smith supported, held that the waste and void Earth and the six days of creation were restricted to the Near East. Another variant of this theory, which G. H. Pember supported, was that the Earth became waste and void because of the great catastrophe that occurred at the time of the Satanic fall. The six days of creation are the restoration of the Earth and have nothing to do with the geological record. The catastrophic events that occurred during the Satanic fall account for much of the geological record. All variants of the Restitution Theory have one thing in common, and that is, an immense indeterminate amount of time elapsed between the creation of the Earth and the six days of creation.

---

*For a more detail discussion of the Framework Theory, see *Studies in Genesis One* by Edward Young, who identifies problems with it, and *The Christian View of the Science and Scripture* by Bernard Ramm, who supports the Pictorial Day Theory.

Some scholars and theologians claim that no gap exists between Genesis 1:1 and 2; it exists before Genesis 1:1. They recognize these two verses as a unit. The three clauses in 1:2 are circumstantial to either verse one or three. Most prefer to identify it with verse one. This precludes a gap between verses one and two. So, another variant to the Restitution Theory has been developed. The gap occurs before the first verse. Thus, Genesis 1:1 describes not the absolute beginning of the heavens and Earth, but a relative beginning. It describes God's creative activity of the Earth later in preparation for man.

The Day-Age Theory

According to the Day-Age Theory, the six days of creation should not be or cannot be regarded as ordinary 24-hour days.* They should be considered as periods of indeterminate length. As these days have an indeterminate length, they can be equated with the vast amount of time required for the geological history of the Earth.

In the first chapter of Genesis, the Hebrew word *yôwm* or *yôm* is translated "day" in the King James Version and most other translations. Fenton translates *yôwm* as "age." The word means day both in the literal sense of from sunrise to sunset or from one sunset to the next or in the figurative sense of a space of time of unspecified duration, era or age. For example, Genesis 2:4

---

*Before the Reformation, the days of Genesis One were not generally interpreted as 24-hour days. Only in the last 400 years have they been interpreted as a literal week of seven consecutive 24-hour days.

reads, "These are the generation of the heavens and of the earth when they were created, in the day that Jehovah God made earth and heaven." Here "day" refers to the entire period described by the six days of creation in chapter one. Even in Genesis One, the word "day" is used in several different senses. In Genesis 1:5 "day" is used as a term for light. It seems to mean a period of 24 hours in Genesis 1:8 and 13. In Genesis 1:14 and 16, it seems to mean a period of 12 hours. As makers of day and night, the Sun and Moon, did not exist until the fourth day. Therefore, the first three days cannot be treated as ordinary days.*

The seventh day is described as God's day of rest. This day has not yet ended and therefore extends a long time. If the seventh day extends a long time, then the preceding six days may also legitimately be considered as long periods of indeterminate length.† It, therefore, cannot be dogmatically asserted that the six days of

---

*Augustine contended that the first three days of creation were not ordinary 24-hour days because they were not marked by the rising and setting of the Sun. The Sun is not specifically mentioned until the fourth day of creation. He said that it was difficult, if not impossible, to conceive the type (or length) of days in these verses. (He also held that the events described in the first two verses of Genesis were not part of the six days of creation.)

† Proof that the seventh day did not end with Genesis 2:3 is that unlike the other six, the Bible does not state that "there was evening and there was morning—the seventh day." The absence of this phrase is one clear indication that the seventh day was never terminated. Hebrews Four provides further support to the continuing existence of God's Sabbath.

Genesis One must be treated as ordinary days. Based on the discoveries of science, the logical and reasonable interpretation of *yôwm* in chapter one would be "era" instead of a literal 24-hour day. Such an interpretation does not infringe upon God's sovereignty or creative powers. Neither does it prove evolution. What seems to finite man as an extremely long time is less than a moment in God's present, which is infinite.*

Further evidence that the days in Genesis One are not 24-hour days, but are days or eras of indeterminate length, is the description of events that occurred on the third and sixth day. Much more than 24 hours is needed for the water to run off from the emerging dry lands on day three. This is especially true if subsequent growth of vegetation also occurred on the same day. For all the events that occurred in the sixth day to occur within 24 hours is impossible. Adam could not have named the multitudes of species of animals that would have existed on that day even if God created them during the first second of the day.

Time is relative. When one looks at the Andromeda galaxy, he sees what happened more than two million years ago. That is, his present is Andromeda's past two million years ago. As Psalm 90:4 puts it, "For a thousand years in thy [God's] sight are but as yesterday when it is past." That a thousand years in man's eyes is but a day in God's shows that God's idea of time differs from man's. That God has a different idea of time is supported by 2 Peter 3:8, which reads, "But forget not this one thing,

---

*Perhaps God created the Universe 15 billion years ago, which is an extremely long time, just to show man how insignificant time is when compared to the eternal God.

beloved, that one day is with the Lord as a thousand years, and a thousand years as one day." Time is relative to the observer. The days in Genesis One are best thought of as days of God and not as 24-hour days.*

Another problem with a literal 24-hour interpretation is how the Hebrews measured the length of a day. To the Hebrews days were measured from sunset to sunset. Thus, a day was seldom 24 hours long. They varied in length. Between the winter solace and the summer solace, each day was the same length or slightly longer than the preceding day. Between the summer solace and the winter solace, each day was the same length or slightly shorter than the preceding day. The length of day would also vary with latitude. Between the summer solace and the winter solace, the farther north or higher the latitude, the longer the day in the northern hemisphere. Several days may pass at the equator while only one day passes above the Arctic Circle where the sun does not set for days.

The creation week of Genesis One is best interpreted as a figurative week with long overlapping days. However, such an interpretation does not mean that the days and the week are allegorical, mythological, or symbolical. What is being described in Genesis One is a historical week, a real week. The events described for the various days are actual events that occurred in space and time. The day-structure is figurative only in the sense that these days are not identical to ordinary 24-hour

---

*In Joel 3:18, Acts 2:20, and John 16:23, "that day" seems to mean the whole Christian era.

days. Rather, they are indeterminate stretches of real, historical time.

Genesis One presents a concise summary of the major events that occurred during the creation week. The general sequence of creation is given, but overlapping of these events is not ruled out. The creation week is described in terms of very broad, large-scale phenomena. It is not described in terms of precise, scientific, technical phenomena (as much as modern man may have wished it to have been so described). Not everything that happened is described. Genesis One is an economy of expression. It is a generalized description of major events.

Creation is just as Divine and miraculous under the long periods allowed under the Day-Age Theory* as it would be if God created the world suddenly and complete. The power necessary to originate and support a ceaseless and prolonged process of developing the world is at least as great as the power necessary to bring it into being in a week.

Six Days of Creation

In the beginning God created the matter that He would use to create planets, stars, and other heavenly bodies as well as the Earth and life forms (Genesis 1:1). This was the creation of the unorganized heaven and Earth. During this initial creation phase, God created the physical laws that would govern the formation of the non-biological aspects of the Universe. This

---

*A more in depth discussion of the Day-Age Theory is found in *Christianity & the Age of the Earth* by Davis Young.

phase included the formation of the stars and other heavenly bodies.

The primitive Earth was then formed out of gaseous material. This gaseous mass solidified. Then water condensed, covered the surface of the Earth, and formed the primeval sea ("the deep"). During this era dense clouds of water vapor and other gases encompassed the Earth. At this stage of development, the Earth was still enveloped with a dense shroud of darkness (Genesis 1:2).*

The light described in Genesis 1:3-5 is not the creation of light or radiant energy as this had been created earlier in Genesis 1:1. What is being described is light on the Earth's surface for the first time. Also, this light must mean more than light from distant stars. Although light from stars can be seen, it does not do away with the darkness and light the Earth.

Several explanations have been offered to explain the mentioning of light during the creation week before the mentioning of the light bearers, the Sun and stars. Many contend that the light referred to in the first day is not the light of the Sun, at least not the light of the Sun as it is presently constituted, because the light of the Sun is not mentioned until the fourth day. This explanation is based upon the fact that the ancient Hebrews believed that light could exist by itself, independently of any luminary. This explanation lacks evidence to support it. Another explanation is that the light being described is that of the original nebula from which, according to the theory of

---

*Genesis 1:2 also shows that "the Spirit of God moved upon [hovered over] the face of the waters," i.e., although the Earth was not yet habitable, all was still under God's control.

Laplace, the entire solar system evolved. This explanation can only be valid if the nebula theory* of the origin of the solar system ultimately proves to be fact. A third explanation is that this light is an electrical light like the light of the Aurora Borealis. Those who believe that the Hebrews derived the initial chapters of Genesis from Babylonian mythology, explain that this light was the "gods of light" from which the "the gods" was omitted in the interest of monotheism. These explanations fail to account satisfactorily for the appearance of light before the appearance of the Sun.

Another explanation, and probably the correct one, is that this light is the light of the Sun. The appearance of sunlight before the appearance of the Sun could have occurred in either of two ways. A dense cloud of water vapor enveloping the Earth prevented the Sun itself from being seen on Earth until the fourth day.† Second if the Earth developed independently of the Sun, then the explanation that a rotating Earth approached the Sun, moved within the gravitational pull, and began to revolve around it is valid. The light of the Sun began to fall on the Earth with enough intensity that a distinction

---

*According to the nebula theory, the matter composing the solar system existed at first in the shape of a vast mass of fiery vapor. This vapor gradually cooled and took the form of a rotating sphere. This sphere threw off the planets. The central part is now the Sun. Thus, light itself could have been regarded as existing before the Sun.

†One reason that Genesis mentions light before the Sun is to turn man away from the Sun as the source of light and towards God as the Creator of light.

between day and night occurred. Accordingly, the light of day and the darkness of night came into being. Either of the latter two explanations or theories, or a combination of them, adequately explain the appearance of light before the appearance of the Sun.

The first day of creation corresponds with the Archeozoic Era. It was the age of rock with no dominant life. Thus, ended the first day or epoch of creation.

The first day faded into the second day as the rain-evaporation cycle came into being. Rain fell to the earth and cooled it. The hot earth quickly evaporated the water. Thus, the Earth was encased with steam until the earth had cooled enough for the primeval seas to form. Next God separated or divided the waters (Genesis 1:6,7). To form the firmament* or atmosphere that divided the waters was the first act. The firmament is the layer of air between the water-covered Earth and clouds above. Part of the water rested on the surface of the Earth and beneath it as groundwater. Part of the water rested above the troposphere, probably as unbroken dense clouds, the canopy, or possibly in the troposphere as ordinary clouds, only perhaps denser and more widespread than

---

*Many believe that Moses thought that the Earth was stationary and covered by a solid dome when he described the Sun and Moon in Genesis 1:14-16 as being placed in the firmament of heaven. However, they error. The "firmament" is not anything "firm;" it is the limitless expanse. In the King James Version, "Firmament" is the translation of the Hebrew word *râqîya'* (Strongs O.T. #7549), which means an expanse, the visible arch of the sky, the heavens. It suggests a finite but unbounded universe. A better translation of *râqîya'* is "expanse," which is found in Fenton's translation and the NIV.

is common today. (Events described on the fourth day supports the canopy theory.)

The second day of creation corresponds with the Proterozoic Era. The creation of single cell life forms began during this era. Thus, ended the second day or epoch of creation.

Then God caused part of the Earth's surface to protrude through the water to form dry land.* The ocean floor sank while land rose to form one or more continents. Genesis 1:9 suggests that surface water was localized.

Once the land had eroded and formed soil, God began the work of making plants† (Genesis 1:12). The early plants were most likely the types of plants suited for a tropical or subtropical, reduced-light environment. More complex life forms, grasses, herbage (vegetables and grains), fruit-bearing trees, are mentioned. Before these more complex plants, God brought forth the simpler plant, such as algae, lichens, fungi, and ferns, that propagated by spores. The implication is that some simpler plants may have been created during the second day. Although plants continued to be created after the third day, the third day is the high point of plant creation. God might have begun creating simpler animal life forms during this era.

The older classification system divides plant life into four basic categories: thallophytes, bryophytes,

---

*The term for "dry land" refers to the continents.

†God also began to create the biological laws of nature on the third day and may not have completed this task until the sixth day when he finished the creation of life forms.

pteridophytes, and spermatophytes. Thallophytes are the lowest form of plant life. They inhabit the water and have no leaf, root, or stem. Algae, bacteria, and fungi are Thallophytes. Genesis 1:9 implies the formation of Thallophytes. Bryophytes are land-hugging and rock-hugging plants. Liverworts and mosses are Bryophytes. These plants live on dry land. Pteridophytes include sporophytes, ferns, club mosses, and horsetails. Genesis 1:10 implies the formation of Bryophytes and Pteridophytes. Spermatophytes are seed plants; they are the flowering and fruit-bearing plants. Genesis 1:11 and 12 describe the formation of these plants.

The third day corresponds with the Silurian, Devonian, and Carboniferous periods. This was the era of plant domination. During the third day, the great coal beds were formed. Thus, ended the third day or epoch of creation.

Genesis 1:14-18 describes the appearance of the Sun, Moon, and stars. Several explanations are offered for the events of the fourth day.

One explanation is that during this epoch seasons begin to appear, i.e., the canopy began to breakup.* A catastrophe may have caused the breakup of the canopy.† The Sun and Moon became visible on the Earth's surface.

---

*Under the canopy theory little variation occurs in climate from one place to another; the global climate is essentially uniform. See the discussion of the Canopy Theory in Chapter 7.

†Perhaps the catastrophe that Patten credits with causing the Flood caused the breakup of the canopy during this epoch instead of during the life of Noah.

(God had created the Sun and Moon during the first day of creation because at the end of the first day light and darkness were present (Genesis 1:3-5). However, because of the canopy, which is described as the second day of creation, the Sun and Moon could not be seen. Only the Sun's effect, light, could be seen.) The seasons, winter and summer, and various climatic zones, arctic, cold deserts, hot deserts, semiarid, temperate, subtropical, tropical, etc., came into being.

Another explanation is that what is being described is the relationship of these bodies to the Earth. It is a description of the present arrangement of the Earth with respect to the Sun and Moon, which does not occur until the fourth day.

Whatever the explanation is, it is not the initial creation or absolute origination of the Sun, Moon, and stars. The origin of heaven and Earth described in Genesis 1:1 occurred at the same time.

During the fourth day the Sun, Moon, and stars, however, began their function as markers of time. Marking time is one of their chief functions. They would later inform man when the time had arrived for religious festivals.

God may have completed the creation of plant life during this era and continued to create animal-life forms. Many, perhaps most, plants need animal life to survive. Worms are needed to aerate the soil. Insects are needed to pollinate* and to help break down dead plant matter.

---

*Some plant species can only be pollinated by one particular insect, which can only survive on that particular plant; thus, both must have been created simultaneously.

The Carboniferous period continued during this day. Thus, ended the fourth day or epoch of creation.

During the fifth day of creation (Genesis 1:20-22), God created* fish, sea creatures of all kinds, birds, and possibly flying insects. Simpler sea creatures may have been created before the fifth day. However, the fifth day was the high point of the creation of fish and birds. The fifth day concludes the Carboniferous period, contains the Permian period, and begins the Mesozoic Era.

During the fifth day, God introduces a new element in the Universe—life. (The ancient world did not consider plant life as true life.) No basis exists in matter or in its products to produce animal life. God had to intervene to fashion (create) this new entity. Thus, ended the fifth day or epoch of creation.

During the sixth day of creation (Genesis 1:24-28), God created the beast of the earth (wild animals, undomesticated mammals),† the cattle (domestic animals), creeping things (short-legged animals like reptiles, amphibians, and insects), and then man (both non-Adamic man and Adamic man). During this epoch one or more catastrophe may have, and probably did, occur that caused the extinction of dinosaurs and many other animals in prehistoric times. The sixth day of

---

*"Create" is the translation of the Hebrew word *bârâ*. It is used three times in Genesis One. It is used for the heavens and Earth, i.e., the Universe. It is used for sea creatures and birds, i.e., animal life, on the fifth day. Finally, it is used for man, i.e., Adam.

†Some believe that the "beast of the earth" refers to the Negro race.

creation ends with God creating Adam and placing him in the Garden of Eden. The sixth day concludes the Mesozoic Era and includes the Cenozoic Era. Thus, ended the sixth day or epoch of creation.

Genesis gives an absolutely correct description of events of creation. The facts of nature agree completely with the account in Genesis. Genesis describes creation as occurring in six stages. Science describes it in six geological stages: Archeozoic (age of rock), Proterozoic (age of protozoa), Paleozoic (age of botanical and aquatic life), Mesozoic (age of reptiles), Cenozoic (age of mammals) and Psychozoic (age of man). Although no human interpretation of Genesis One is infallible, the Day-Age Theory with long successive overlapping days of creation most closely approximates the truth.

Why Describe Creation as Occurring in Six Days?

Gaunt offers this explanation for describing creation as occurring in six days: Six is a perfect number.* A correct explanation is that six days of creation work followed by a seventh day of rest stresses the importance of the Sabbath.

Perhaps the primary reason for describing creation as six days of creative work followed by the seventh day of rest is to emphasize the fourth commandment: "remember the Sabbath day, to keep it holy. Six days shalt thou labor, and do all thy work; but the seventh day

---

*A perfect number is an integer whose factors, excluding the number itself, when summed equals the number. Another perfect number is 28.

is a Sabbath unto Jehovah thy God: in it thou shalt not work . . . for in six days Jehovah made heaven and earth, the sea, and all that in them is, and rested the seventh day: wherefore Jehovah blessed the Sabbath day, and hallowed it." The creation week serves to guide man in his week. Man is to work six days of the week because God worked six days.* Man is to rest one day of the week because God rested one day. Thus, the creation week is the Divine prototype of the human week. Man's seven day week is a copy of this Divine week.

---

*God performed His task of creation in six days and then rested from His creative work. He continues today His work of sustaining and governing His universe.

3
CREATION OF MAN

Creationists who are monogenists argue that all the races of men descended from Adam or Noah. They claim that sin caused the genes or DNA of Adam and his descendants to deteriorate and become defective, which is true. From this fact they jump to the conclusion that this deterioration led to the formation of the races of men. Like begat unlike.

Thus, their disagreement with evolutionists is not over the concept of like begetting unlike, but over the direction. Evolutionists believe that the higher races of men evolved or developed from a more primitive race. The creationists believe the reverse: The more primitive races developed or evolved from the higher race. Both agree that A (Negroes, Turanians, etc.) descended from B (proto-man). Their disagreement is whether A is the superior form or B is the superior form. The evolutionists claim A is superior to B while the traditional creationists claim that B is superior to A.*

---

*Whether they admit it, or even know it, the theories of both make the Negro race inferior to the Aryan race. Many evolutionists claim that Africa is the original home of man. In an attempt to degrade the White man, they claim that this early man was closely akin to the Negro. From Africa groups or tribes, early man migrated to Eurasia where they evolved into

The polygenetic theory of creation does not require any race to be inferior to another. This theory holds that God created each race for a specific zoological niche. He placed the races either directly or, more often, indirectly via migration in the niche for which He designed them. Disease, temperature, and other environmental factors helped regulate their movement. Racial prejudice, which God gave each race, helped to keep them from committing the sin of miscegenation.

Monogenesis or Polygenesis

Monogenesis and polygenesis are the two basic concepts of the origin of the races of men. Monogenesists claim that all of the races of men are descended from a common single origin or set of parents. Polygenesists claim that the races of men, like the different species of animals, have separate origins and are descended from different ultimate ancestors.

---

the Aryan and Turanian races of today. According to the theory of evolution, higher forms descended from lower forms. Therefore, the Aryan race, which descended from proto-Negro, must be superior to the Negro race.

The traditional creationists claim that all the races descended from Adam. Adam was white. According to the traditional creationist evolutionist theory, lower forms descend from higher forms. Therefore, the Negro race, which descended from the Aryan race, must be inferior to the Aryan race.

Nearly all evolutionists* and creationists are monogenesists. Evolutionists claim that all the races of men have a common origin. The races of men have evolved from the same primitive form. Nearly all creationists claim that all the races of men have a common origin. The races of men have descended from a single pair, Adam and Eve.

If the monogenetic theory is true, evolution must have occurred because the races of men are uniquely different. To account for the diversity of the races of men, the monogenetic concept requires evolutionary changes. Monogenesis is the very essence of the theory of evolution: All life is descended from one original life-form. The great irony is that the creationists who believe monogenesis are the very ones who are the most vigorous in refuting evolutionary views.

A. H. Keane exposes the monogenetic traditional creationists for the evolutionists that they are. He wrote,

> But the supernatural view can in no way get rid of evolution, which is indispensable to any theory that attempts to account for many patent facts in the natural history of the Hominidae [i.e., man]. It is not, for instance, pretended that all the Hominidae were

---

*Actually all evolutionists are ultimately monogenesists. Some evolutionists, such as C. S. Coon, place the origin of the races of men prior to *Homo sapiens*. However, they do place the origin in some common ancestor. Coon, for instance, places the origin of the several races of men in *Homo erectus*. According to Coon's theory, the races of men that appear in *Homo sapiens* actually developed and came into being in *Homo erectus*. Only in a limited sense could evolutionists like Coon be considered polygenesists.

independently created, but one only. Consequently the transition from, say, the Homo Caucasicus [i.e., Aryan] (if he was the starting-point) to the Homo Æthiopicus [i.e., Negro], must have been effected by some natural evolutionary process; from this there is no escape for the creationist. Now the typical white man differs enormously from the typical Negrito, so much so that they would have to be regarded as separate species but for the intermediate forms in actual existence. Here then we have in any case a range of evolution scarcely less than that which is covered by the transition from Gibbon to Orang to Chimpanzee. The difference is obviously one of degree only, and not of kind, so far as regards physical structure.*

That evolutionists are monogenesists is understandable. But why are nearly all creationists monogenesists? The answer must be that monogenesis supports their doctrine of the unity of man and equality of the races. Hence, they subordinate science and Scripture to support their egalitarian dogma. Without a common origin of the races, their egalitarian dogma falls.

Unlike the monogenetic theory, the polygenetic theory agrees with science and the Scriptures. Genetics, culture, language, and the Holy Scriptures all support the polygenetic origins of the species of men.

Supporters of the unity of man claim that the various types of man should be classified as one species because the diversities that exist "pass into each other by insensible gradations or degrees." This principle is never equally applied to animal taxonomy. Because exact lines

---

*A. H. Keane, *Ethnology* (Cambridge, 1896), p. 29.

of distinction cannot always be drawn in the races of men is no reason for classifying them as one species. The same gradation occurs throughout the whole animal kingdom. Such gradation has not prevented classifying the animal kingdom into numerous species rather than one species.

Advocates of the doctrine of the unity of man are fond of emphasizing the ability of the various races of men to interbreed as proof that the races of men belong to the same species. However, the fact of human hybrids does not prove that all humans are of the same species or should be regarded as such. The reason that these people stress the importance of hybridity in classifying all the races of men as one species is that little else in the scientific or physical realm supports their doctrine.

When classifying types as a species or a variety, the fact of whether reproduction can or cannot take place between the two types should not be the only criteria used. What should be used is whether or not they naturally reproduce in nature. The intent of the Creator and the guidelines established by His laws should be the guidelines used to decide what a species is. There are animals classified as different species and even different genera that are mutually fertile when bred.* The weight

---

*Fertile offspring are produced when cattle (*Bos taurus*) are interbred with zebu (*Bos indicus*). A dog (*Canis familiaris*) bred with a wolf (*Canis lupus*), a jackal (*Canis aureus*), or a dingo (*Canis dingo*) produce fertile offspring. A goat (*Capra hircus*) bred with a sheep (*Ovis aries*) or an aoudad (*Ammotragus lervia*) produces fertile offspring.

of scientific evidence seems to justify classifying the various races of men as distinct species.*

Further, the survival rate of hybrids in man is less than non-hybrids. The prenatal mortality of offspring of parents, one of whom is Aryan and the other Negro, exceeds those whose parents are of the same race. This excess mortality seems independent of socioeconomic status. The male sex ratio is noticeably lower from these interracial matings. Fewer male children are born from interracial matings than occur when both parents are of the same race. Hence, interracial matings are not as natural as the monogenesists would argue.

Separate origin and distinctness of race evinced by a constant transmission of some characteristic peculiarity of organization are the key criteria. A race of animal showing peculiar characteristics that are constantly displayed is a "species." Two races are specifically different if they are distinguished from each other by some characteristic for which there is no evidence of it having been acquired by one or lost by the other through known operation of physical causes.

The races of men are so distinct that if they were any other animals they would be classified as different species—perhaps even as different genera. The reason that they are not classified as different species is that

---

*The reason that the several races of men, unlike other species that can produce fertile offspring, are inclined to interbreed is SIN. Man is naturally a sinner. His nature is to rebel against God and God's laws. He is naturally inclined towards the forbidden fruit of miscegenation. For this reason God has endowed man with "racial prejudice" to retard this sin.

such classification is contrary to the socialistic doctrine of the unity of man and racial equality.

Atheist Voltaire was more of an anti-evolutionist than most creationists. He believed that different characteristics of the various human races were hereditary and immutable. Ignoring the laws of genetics, traditional creationists reject heredity and immutability by claiming that the Yellow race and Black race evolved from the White race.*

Many traditional creationists, like many evolutionists, claim that environment has caused the races and has determined their attributes. The environmental origin of the races leaves much to be desired. If environment were the primary factor in determining racial characteristics, then all, or at least most, people living in the same type of environment would have similar racial characteristics. They do not. Turanians live in environments similar to those in which Aryans and Negroes live. Yet they are distinct from these two races.

No real evidence exists about one race ever transforming into another race throughout recorded history, or even earlier for that matter. If all the races of men developed (or evolved) from Noah as many creationists claim, the Aryans who settled in South Africa more than four hundred years ago have had time at least to begin to develop into Negroes or Khoisans. No one has yet seen any signs of this transformation.

---

*In Jeremiah 13:23, the Scriptures affirm the heredity and immutability of the races.

Environment does not determine race and has little effect on racial attributes. Environment can determine which race has the highest probability of surviving. The attributes of one race may give it an advantage over other races in a given location or environment. For example, Negroes are superior to Aryans in surviving in the tropics because of higher tolerance for ultraviolet light as well as other innate physiological reasons. Studies intended to show that races are the result of adaptation or environment really show that one race is more suitable for a given environment than others. The most suitable race for a particular environment will tend to dominate while others will decline in that environment.

Creationists who are of the unity of man school but are not of the Lamarck school* use the evolutionist concept of natural selection to explain the races of men.† According to these creationists, Noah's children and their wives possessed all the genes necessary to form the several races of men. Hence, they were hybrids or as they generally prefer to say "heterozygotes." Somehow this motley group of mongrels split into isolated groups. For some unexplained reason, each of these groups just happened to possess the genetic makeup for one race, but they lacked the genes to produce the other races. These groups naturally knew what sort of environment was best

---

*Lamarck believed that environment determined the attributes of a species. For example, a group of men with light skin color exposed to the tropical Sun over many generations will eventually produce children with dark skins.

†Nelson briefly presents the natural selection argument in *After Its Kind*.

suited for its particular set of genes and instinctively migrated to that environment. As Mount Ararat of Turkey (according to the most common creationist theories) was the most likely center of such outward migration, neither the Aryans nor Turanians had to migrate. Yet for some unexplained reason the Turanians migrated thousands of miles eastward. Further, Negroes found themselves in a hostile environment. They had to survive long enough in this hostile environment to develop and to migrate thousands of miles to the tropics. Such is the argument of many creationists. Such is the argument of many evolutionists.

The scientific evidence shows that racial characteristics are permanent and have always been permanent. Although speculations abound that one race evolved into another, no real evidence of this happening exists. The laws of genetics are against its happening. Such permanence of characteristics is the surest test of a species.

The Scriptures offer little or no support for this speculative hypothesis. A purpose of the Flood was to destroy a mongrel population, which proves that Noah's sons and their wives were not mongrels. The natural selection hypothesis offered by traditional creationists is false and invalid. A much better and simpler explanation of the origin of the races of men is special creation of each primary race. God created each race (or species) of man independently at a different time and in a different place. The Scriptures support the hypothesis of special creation of each race.

The creation model used by the traditional creationists is in error. Their model is a monogenetic model and is based on the principle that God created only a general type or kind of each animal and plant. All the various species derived, developed, or descended— that is evolved—from these few original types.

The model of traditional creationists is nothing more than an evolutionist model in disguise. The primary difference is that under the traditional evolutionist model the species develop over millions of years. Under the traditional creationist model, species develop over a few generations. The Bible and the laws of genetics condemn both models, for like begets like.

When nature (God's work) is interpreted in light of the Scriptures (God's word) and when the Scriptures are interpreted in light of nature, no conflict between science and the Bible exists. Instead there is harmony.

E. B. Taylor in his article "Anthropology" in the *Encyclopedia Britannica* sums up the problem faced by the traditional creationists with their monogenetic model,

> But although the reality of some such modification is not disputed, especially as to stature and constitution, its amount is not enough to upset the counter proposition of the remarkable permanence of type displayed by races ages after they have been transported to climates extremely different from that of their former home. Moreover, physically different races, such as the Bushmen and the Negroids in Africa, show no signs of approximation under the influence of the same climate; while, on the other hand, the coast tribes of Terra del Fuego and forest tribes of tropical Brazil continue to resemble one another. Mr. Darwin, than whom no naturalist could be more competent to appraise the variation of species, is moderate in his estimation of the changes produced in races of men by climate and mode of life

within the range of history. The slightness and slowness of variation in human races having become known, a great difficulty of the monogenetic theory was seen to lie in the shortness of the chronology with which it was formerly associated. Inasmuch as several well-marked races of mankind, such as the Egyptians, Phoenicians, Ethiopians, etc., were much the same three or four thousand years ago as now, their variation from a single stock in the course of any like period could hardly be accounted for without a miracle. This difficulty was escaped by the polygenetic theory.*

Their natural response is "a miracle did occur—by a miracle Noah's descendants were converted into the several species of men." They can offer no evidence of such a miracle. If such a miracle did occur, the Bible surely would have mentioned it. About such a miracle, the Bible is silent. The claim for such a miracle rests solely on wild speculation with no evidence to support it. Nothing supports it, but the doctrine of the unity of man.

A polygenetic model is the correct model. It is based on the special creation of each species and race of man. Under this model, no need for evolution exists. Further, it harmonizes with science and the Scriptures.

Traditional creationists fail because they ignore or try to explain away God's work instead of trying to harmonize it with God's word. Evolutionists fail because they ignore God's word.

---

*[William H. Campbell], *Anthropology for the People: A Refutation of the Theory of the Adamic Origin of All Races.* (Richmond, 1891), p. 148.

The correct interpretation of God's word (the Bible) and God's work (nature) is the polygenetic model. God created each race independently at a different time, in a different location, and with different original parents. Such an interpretation harmonizes the Scriptures and science and annihilates evolution.

The debate between traditional creationists and evolutionists is really superficial. Their purpose is to obfuscate. They offer people a false dichotomy by contriving a conflict between the Scriptures and science. They will do anything to protect their false doctrine of the unity of man and the equality of the races. Whichever theory or model one chooses, the result is the same: The races of men evolved (descended, developed) from one common stock. At all cost the Goddess of Equality* must be protected. The truth must be concealed. The truth is that the races of men are different. They are, therefore, unequal. They do not have a common origin other than God created them independently at different times and places.

Pre-Adamic Men

Before He created Adam, God created several other species of men. Five of these species are extant today. They are the Khoisans, Australians, Negroes, Turanians, and Melanochroi.

When God created a species that depends on sexual reproduction, at a minimum He must have created a male and female of the species. For most species He probably

---

*Egalitarianism is contrary to the Scriptures. The Bible teaches the inequality of man.

created multiple males and females. Further, for species like those that can and do interbreed, He had to isolate them from each other until their population had built up. If they were allowed to crossbreed indiscriminately, their unique and distinguishing characteristics could be lost.

Australians and Khoisans were the first species of modern man whom God created. They were created about 75,000 years ago* during the latter part of the Riss-Würm interglacial period. Australians were probably created on the Anatolian Plateau. Khoisans were created somewhere in what is now the Sahara Desert.

Three of the great divisions of man, Black, Yellow, and Brown, were created during the Laufen interglacial period. Between the end of the Würm I glaciation and the peak of the Würm II glaciation, God created three more species of man, Negroes, Turanians, and Melanochroi. The most probable date of their creation is about 55,000 years ago. Negroes were created on the Deccan Plateau of India. Turanians were created on the Tibetan Plateau. Melanochroi were created on the Iranian Plateau.

God created the Khoisans somewhere on what is now the Sahara Desert, which was not a desert then, about 75,000 years ago. From their place of origin, they spread

---

*The dates that follow are obviously approximations. The creation and migration of the several species of men relate closely to glacial and interglacial periods. However, authorities disagree over when these periods began and ended. A change in the dating of the beginning or ending of glacial and interglacial periods can change the dating of creation and migration of one or more of the species of man. In general the dates before the first millennium B.C. are probably within plus or minus ten percent.

across northern Africa until they ranged from the Atlantic along the slopes of the Atlas Mountains to the Nile. They may have even entered Europe. With the arrival of the Negroes in eastern Africa and later the Melanochroi in northern Africa, the Khoisans began their migration to southern Africa.

God created the Australians about 75,000 years ago on the Anatolian Plateau. From here they spread westward into Europe and eastward into Iran. Most of those who left their Anatolian homeland settled in Mesopotamia and Iran with some even reaching East Asia. By the time that they began migrating from western Asia, they had acquired the Mousterian culture from the neighboring Neanderthals. During the Würm I glaciation, they migrated eastward and southward in search of a warmer climate. Many had reached India* by the end of the Würm I glaciation (c. 57,000 B.P.†) where they spread across the Indo-Gangetic Plain. Here they remained until the Negroes drove them out.

As Negroes moved into the Ganges valley, they drove the Australians living there into Burma. (These were the progenitors of today's Australians.) As Negroes moved westward across the Indo-Gangetic Plain, they drove the remaining Australians into the Deccan and down the west coast of India or to the Chota Plateau. (This group became the progenitors of the Pre-Dravidians.) Later the Melanochroi drove most of the Pre-Dravidians farther

---

*In this book India includes modern-day India, Pakistan, and Bangladesh.

†B.P. means before the present. It is about 2000 years more than B.C.

south into the coastal lands and jungles of southern India and other places that the Melanochroi found as undesirable habitats.

The Australians who fled to Burma migrated down the Malay Peninsula into Indonesia. These Australians were the Wadjak man from whom today's Australians descended. For the next several thousand years, they were continually pushing them southward and eastward by Negro tribes. By the peak of the Würm II glaciation (c. 45,000 B.P.), some Australians had spread across Indonesia into New Guinea.

God created the Negroes about 55,000 years ago on the Deccan Plateau. Gradually they left the Deccan. From the Deccan they migrated to the Ganges valley, which was hotter and more humid than the Deccan, because they found its climate more pleasurable. As their population grew in the Ganges valley, the Negroes began to spread westward across the Indo-Gangetic Plain.

Shortly before or with the onset of the Würm II glaciation (c. 50,000 B.P.), hordes of Dravidian Melanochroi crossed the Sulaiman Mountains and drove nearly all Negroes from India. A few Negro tribes fled to Burma. Most fled along the coast of the Arabian Sea into Iran. Here more Melanochroi pressed them from the north. These Negroes crossed into southern Arabia. After traveling across southern Arabia, they entered Africa. Their migration must have been slow, for they do not appear to have settled in Africa much before 40,000 B.P.

The Negroes driven into Burma spread across Farther India. About 24,000 years ago the Dravidians drove many of them from Farther India down the Malay Peninsula across the East Indies into New Guinea. The Negritos of

Malaya, Indonesia, and the Philippines and the Melanesians are the descendants of these Negroes.

God created the Melanochroi about 55,000 years ago on the Iranian Plateau. As their numbers grew, they began to migrate away from the Iranian Plateau.

One branch or racial type, the Dravidians, crossed the Sulaiman Mountains shortly before or with the onset of the Würm II glaciation and drove nearly all the Negroes from India. After driving the Negroes from India, Melanochroic control of northern India was forever established. India is today the land of the Melanochroi.

As the Würm II glaciation began to advance, the changing climate forced most Melanochroi remaining on the Iranian Plateau to search for a more hospitable climate. Some emigrated to the southern shores of the Caspian Sea. Others emigrated to Lower Mesopotamia.

With the end of the Würm II glaciation, Melanochroic people known as the Grimaldi race entered Europe. After entering Europe, they established the Aurignacian culture*(c. 35,000 B.P.) While the Grimaldi race was settling in Europe, other Melanochroi settled in East Africa.

Between the Würm II and Würm III glaciation the population of Melanochroi also grew rapidly in northeastern Iran. During the Würm III advance (28,000 to 22,000 B.P.), the population of the Melanochroi covered much of the Iranian Plateau and adjacent lands. In the southwest lived the Cro-Magnards. The progenitors

---

*The Aurignacian culture was a European culture characterized by pressure-flaked points and tanged points and lasted from about 35,000 to 30,000 years ago.

of the Eastern-Hamites, Saharan-Hamites, and Egyptians occupied the southern region. In eastern Iran were the Indo-Iranians. Dravidians lived in Baluchistan and along the coast of the Arabian Sea.

As the Würm III glaciation advanced, coldness forced the people of northwestern Iran who had migrated from Europe southward. They in turned pushed the Melanochroic Cro-Magnards through Syria toward the Mediterranean Sea and finally to North Africa. Migrating across North Africa, they crossed into Europe at Gibraltar about 23,000 years ago. They established the Magdalenian culture* in Europe. As the Cro-Magnards spread across Europe, their culture soon became the predominate culture of Europe.

With the retreat of the Würm III glaciation, the Melanochroi who were living south of the Caspian Sea migrated into Europe as the Brünn race and established the Solutrean culture† about 20,000 years ago. They settled in the Danube River valley. From here, their culture spread into Ukraine, Moravia, Poland, Bavaria, and France.

Between 20,000 and 15,000 years ago, Melanochroi moved into Mesopotamia and spread from the Nafud to the southern shores of the Black Sea. They gradually migrated westward into Upper Egypt and then along the

---

*The Magdalenian culture was characterized by reindeer-hunting and the manufacture of unretouched blades and bones and antler tools.

†The Solutrean culture was characterized by finely worked laurel-leaf points and long, pressure-flaked bifacial blade tools.

northern coast of Africa. These Melanochroi were progenitors of the Saharan-Hamites. About 15,000 years ago they moved across and settled along northern Africa in large numbers. By 10,000 B.C. their settlements were scattered along both sides of the Mediterranean Sea.

God created the Turanians about 55,000 years ago on the Tibetan Plateau. With the beginning of the Würm II glaciation (c. 50,000 B.P.), large numbers of Turanians moved down the eastern slopes of the plateau. The headwaters of the Irrawaddy, Salween, Mekong, Yangtze (Blue River), and Hwang (Yellow River) now became the region of their growth and dispersal. As the glaciation advanced, they moved down the river valleys and into western China. They spread from Szechwan and Yunnan provinces of southwest China into Farther India. In search of more favorable habitats, some traveled as far as the coastal plains.

As the Würm II glaciation retreated (c. 35,000 B.P.), Turanians spread across China. Other Turanians migrated into the Tibetan highlands. A few thousand years later, Turanians were settling western China and Mongolia.

About 22,000 years ago, the first wave of Turanians to enter North America crossed into Alaska. They gradually moved down the Mackenzie River. About a millennium after leaving Asia, they had settled in the north-central plains of America. By 20,000 B.P. they had reached the Peruvian Andes. Other tribes of Turanians entered North America between 17,000 and 14,000 years ago and had reached the Andes of South America between 14,000 and 12,000 years ago. Beginning about 8000 B.C., another wave of Turanians spread to North America.

About 8000 B.C. Turanian Turks expanded into western Tibet. Some Turks traversed the mountains into the Tarim Basin of Eastern Turkestan, which was much less arid than it is today. For nearly the next five thousand years the Turanians, primarily Turks, and Aryans would contend for the Tarim Basin until the Flood destroyed all the inhabitants of the basin except Noah and his family. It was to these Turks that Cain fled and founded the Cainite empire. He brought these Turks the superior technology of the Neolithic culture.*

Creation of Adam

The last species of men whom God created was Adam, the father of the Aryans. Adam was created about 8,100 B.C. on the Pamir Plateau. With Genesis 1:27 begins the cultural history of man with the creation of Adam.

Genesis 1:26 reads, "And God said, Let us make man in our image, after our likeness: and let them have dominion over . . . all the earth." The Hebrew word in this verse translated "man" is *'âdâm*. This word is translated "Adam" in the second chapter of Genesis. More than five hundred times *'âdâm* is translated Adam. If this word had been translated "Adam" instead of "man," there would be no doubt that the Bible deals only with the Adamic race. The Adamic, Aryan or White race, is the

---

*For more details about the migrations of Pre-Adamic man, see *Races of Mankind: Their Origin and Migration* by Calvin Kephart.

race created in the likeness of God and given dominion over the earth.*

A more literal and correct translation of Genesis 1:26 and 27 is "... God said, Let us make Adam ('âdâm) in our image, after our likeness ... And God created the Adam [or, the Adamite](ha- 'âdâm) in his own image ...." This translation clearly shows that Adam and the Adamite are the race whom God created in His own image. If the traditional translation of 'âdâm as man is used, these verse should read, "... Let us make *a man* in our image ... And God created *the man* in his own image...." Such a literal translation clearly shows that a particular man is being created, not mankind in general. This record of Adam's creation strongly suggests the existence of other races of men at the time of his creation.

God created the Adamic race to "have dominion over all the earth." He created the Adamic race to civilize mankind. As shown below, the Adamic race is the source of civilization. He exalted this race, and other races have recognized it as God's chosen (Acts 13:17). God also chose the Adamic race as the race from which He would bring His Son, who would be man's savior.

The Scriptures do not claim that Adam was the first man or that he is the father of all the races of man. To the contrary the Scriptures present evidence that other people already existed before Adam was created.

When God placed Adam in the Garden of Eden, He gave Adam two duties to perform. First he was to tend or

---

*Some distinguish between the creation of man in Genesis One and the creation of Adam in Genesis Two. The creation described in Genesis One is pre-Adamic man. That described in Genesis Two is Adam himself, the father of the Aryan race.

dress the Garden of Eden. Second he was to protect (keep) it.

The word translated "keep" in the King James Version is *shâmar*, (Strongs O.T. #8104), which means "to hedge about (as with thorns), i.e., guard; generally to protect, attend to, etc." Although most versions translate this word as "keep," the Amplified Bible translates it as "guard and keep," and Moffatt translates it as "guard." Those who translate *shâmar* as "keep," translate it in the sense of preserving, watching over, and defending if they translate it according to the root meaning of the word.

From whom was Adam to defend the Garden of Eden? His enemy appeared not to be wildlife, for God brought them to Adam to name. That he was to defend it from Satan is also unlikely. God would not have asked Adam to protect the Garden of Eden from a being more powerful than he. The Bible clearly illustrates that man lacks the power to protect himself, much less anything else, from Satan. (He must rely solely on the power of God for such protection.) So who was the enemy from whom Adam was to guard the Garden? The most logical answer is that he was to defend it from other men—most likely the ones to whom Cain fled in Nod.

Another indication that the world was well populated at the time that Cain slew Abel is that Cain lured Abel into the countryside to kill him. He goes into the countryside away from any population center, so no one would witness his murder. If the only people on Earth were Adam, Eve, Cain, and Able and an unnamed daughter with whom Cain could flee, as the traditionalists claim, Cain would not need to take his brother into the country to kill him.

Furthermore, in Genesis 4:14 Cain claimed that he would be a fugitive and expressed fear that anyone who found him would slay him. Whom did Cain have to fear if Adam and Eve were the only people alive at that time? From whom would he be a fugitive? No evidence is given by the Bible that Adam and Eve had another child until after Cain had fled. Even if they did, Cain had no more reason to fear his brothers and sisters than his parents—perhaps even less fear since, according to the traditionalists, he married one of his sisters. Cain was not expressing fear of his family. He was expressing fear about people of other races who existed before Adam's creation. God affirmed this conclusion in His response to Cain in Genesis 4:15 when He told Cain, "Therefore whosoever slayeth Cain, vengeance shall be taken on him sevenfold." Then He placed a mark on Cain. God was acknowledging that many other people were then living who could have slain Cain and that He would avenge Cain's death if any of them slew him. If only Adam and Eve were living, and some brothers and sisters as the traditionalists claim, what purpose would the "mark " have served? After all, his parents knew their own son. If he had any siblings at the time of his flight, surely they knew their own brother. The "mark" was so that the other people then living could recognize that Cain was under God's protection. Cain was certainly aware that other people were then living who would delight in killing him.

Genesis 4:17 provides more evidence that Adam and Eve were not the first man and woman. This verse shows that Cain found a wife, who bore his children. If Adam and Eve were the only people at this time, then how was Cain able to find a wife? No evidence is given in the Scriptures that Adam and Eve had any daughters to whom Cain could marry at the time the Bible describes Cain's marriage. In fact Adam and Eve do not appear to have had any daughters until well after Cain's marriage. His marriage, the birth of his son Enoch, and his building of a city all occur before Eve gave birth to Seth. According to the Bible, Adam and Eve had no daughters until after Seth's birth.

The conventional explanation for Cain's wife is that he married his sister. If Cain's wife was a daughter of Adam, why should she be punished along with Cain for a crime of which she was innocent? Why should she be banished along with him and forever separated from her parents? Why should her children be denied proper religious training and righteous rearing? The answer to these questions is that Cain's wife was not a daughter of Adam. Scriptural evidence that Adam and Eve had any daughters for Cain to marry at the time the Bible describes his marriage is lacking.

Cain did not marry his sister. He married a woman of another race, probably a Turanian. Jude supports the belief that Cain married outside his race. In verses five through eleven, Jude condemns old and new apostates. He compares the new apostates with the old. The most common sin that he identifies with the old apostates is the sin of miscegenation. In verse seven he states that Sodom and Gomorrah had "given themselves over to sexual immorality and gone after strange flesh." That is, they lusted after people of a different race. In verse eleven he states the apostates had "gone in the way of Cain" and had followed "the error of Balaam." The error of Balaam was his advice to Balak, King of Moab, to destroy Israel by having his mongrel people integrate with the Israelites and intermarry with them. Using Cain's name in parallel with Balaam, Jude strongly suggests that both of them were guilty of the same sin, miscegenation.

Further evidence that the world was populated at the time God created Adam, is that Cain built his son Enoch a city (Genesis 4:17). The building of a city certainly implies the presence of a large population. Even if this city were no more than a village of huts as some commentators claim, it still implies a population much larger than would have been the case if all mankind were descended from Adam and Eve. The building of a city strongly suggests that the land to which Cain fled was already inhabited. Why would he bother building a city if the area to which he fled was uninhabited? The dwelling that he, his wife, and son had would surely have sufficed.

In an attempt to prove that Adam was the first man of all mankind created and the father of all races, theologians who preach the doctrine of the unity of man quote Genesis 3:20, 1 Corinthians 15:45, Acts 17:26, and Galatians 3:28, Romans 10:12, and Colossians 3:11. None of these verses, however, support their claims.

Quoting Genesis 3:20 (". . . Eve . . . was the mother of all living"), these theologians claim that Eve is the mother of all the species of men. As discussed in detail in the chapter on the Flood, "all" does not always mean the whole number of or every last one. It frequently means many or a large number. In this passage Eve is being called the mother of the Aryan race, the mother of all Adam's descendants. She is the mother of all with whom the Bible is concerned, i.e., the Aryans. Expressions like this one that appear to refer to all the inhabitants of the Earth, nearly always only refer to those created in God's image, i.e., Adam's descendants, the Aryans.

These theologians are fond of quoting the first half of 1 Corinthians 15:45: "So it is written, The first man Adam became a living soul." Then they argue that all men are descended from Adam. They overlook the last half of the verse: "The last Adam became a live-giving spirit." They omit it because it makes no sense considering their doctrine. It immediately raises the question: Who is the last Adam? (The answer, of course, is Jesus Christ, with which nearly all, if not all, theologians agree.) The correct reading of this passage is that Adam was the first man of the Adamic line, not of all the racial lines existing today. Then the answer that Jesus Christ is the last Adam becomes clear. Jesus was born out of Adam through Abraham, Judah, and David. Verse 47 supports this conclusion: "The first man [Adam] is of the earth, earthly: the second man [Christ] is of heaven." Adam was the "first man" only in the same sense that Christ was the "second" man. Adam was the figure of Christ (Romans 5:14). If these verses are to be interpreted consistently, they cannot be understood as describing Adam in a physical sense. If they are referring to Adam in a physical sense, then Jesus was, according to verse 45, the last man, which is absurd. These verses outline a basic theme of the Bible: death in Adam, life in Christ. This is the light in which these verses should be understood—not as proof that Adam fathered all the races of men.

Perhaps the favorite verse of the preachers of the doctrine of the unity of man is Acts 17:26: "And he [God] hath made of one blood all nations of men for to dwell on all the face of the earth, and hath determined the times before appointed, and the bounds of their habitation." This is the *King James Version*. The *American Standard Version*, *New American Standard Version*, *Revised*

Standard Version, Berkeley Version,★ and *The Holy Bible in Modern English* translated by Ferrar Fenton† omit the word "blood." Weymouth in his *New Testament in Modern English* gives in a footnote the literal translation, "from one," and notes that "from one blood" is an alternative reading found in some manuscripts. "One blood" appears only in some later manuscripts and, therefore, probably is not in the original.

This verse does not prove that all the races of men descended from Adam. It does show that God created each race of man. He created them at different times or by "the times before appointed." He placed each of them in their own specific zoological zone or geographical area ("bounds of their habitation").

The preachers of the doctrine of the unity of man also like to quote Galatians 3:28, Romans 10:12, or Colossians 3:11: "Where there is neither Greek nor Jew." The Jew and Greek referred to in these verses are both descendants of Adam. They are both Aryans. These verses are referring to one race, the Aryan race, living in different countries and conditions being united under Christ. They do not prove the doctrine of the unity of man.

Thus, the verses often quoted to support the doctrine that all races of men descended from Adam fail to support this doctrine. Only the White race descended from Adam.

★In a footnote the *Berkeley Version* identifies the word "one" as being God.

†Fenton capitalizes "one" to show that it refers to God.

What Race Was Adam?

Adam was created White.* The name "adam" is *'âdâm* in Hebrew and means a "ruddy human being" (Strong's O.T. #120). It is derived from "adam" (Strong's O.T. #119), or *'âdam* in Hebrew, which means "to show blood (in the face), i.e., flush or turn rosy." Only one race has the characteristic of blushing or showing blood in the face or skin, and that race is the White or Aryan race.

Adam was named "Adam" because he possessed a ruddy or rosy complexion. He was fair and White and, therefore, the hemoglobin showed through his nonpigmented skin giving a ruddy or flush look. His name described his physical appearance. It is a physical characteristic that appears only in the White race.

The Bible further proves that Adam and Eve were of the White race with fair and ruddy or rosy complexion by the way it describes their descendants. 1 Samuel 16:12 and 17:47 describe David as being "ruddy and of fair complexion." 2 Samuel 13:1 describes David's daughter, Tamar, as "fair." Genesis 12:11 and 14 describe Sarah as "very fair," and Genesis 24:16 and 26:7 describes Rebekah as "very fair." They are descendants of Adam. In Songs of Solomon 5:10, Solomon is said to be "white and ruddy." In Lamentations 4:7 the Nazarites (consecrated persons)

---

*To support his theory that all of the races of men descended from Adam and Eve, Nelson claimed that Adam and Eve were motley mongrels (he calls them mulattoes). But God is not the author of confusion. Therefore, Adam and Eve could not have been mongrels.

of Judah are described as "whiter than milk" and "more ruddy in body than rubies."*

Adam and Eve were White. The church has historically always depicted them as White and correctly so. As recorded in the Bible, Adam's descendants end up being White or at least of a light complexion. This is a fact that no one seriously denies. Yet traditional creationists also claim that all the other races are also descended from Adam.†

Adam was not the father of the human race. He is only the father of the Aryan race. Each race is a distinct and separate creation. God created each race independently of the others and at different times. Hence, each race is a distinct species.

Scientific evidence suggests a high antiquity of man along with evidence of definite anatomical differences. Each race of man is descended from a different human pair whom God created with different external and internal characteristics.

The Scriptures and science agree. The fossil record supports the Bible, and the Bible supports the fossil record. Adam was not the first human that God created.

---

*Throughout the Scriptures "white" and "light" are used to symbolize honor, purity, goodness, and other Godly attributes. Black, dark, or colored are used in the Scriptures to symbolize that which is evil or corrupt or that which brings misery.

†See *The Origin of Race and Civilization* by Charles A. Weismen and *Tracing Our White Ancestors (White Roots)* by Frederick Haberman for further proof of that only the White race descended from Adam.

Adam was only the first individual of a new species, the Aryan race of man.

Although traditional creationists and evolutionists view each other's theories with enmity, their theories have much in common. Both claim that all races of men have a common origin. Both claim that early man possessed a wide variety of genetic traits that allow for the different races. Both claim that only minor variations exist among the races today. Both claim that the races are the result of climate, environment, natural selection, and group isolation. Both claim one species, race, or kind can produce others—the principle of speciation. Both claim that God did not create the individual races of men. Both claim that no pure race exists because gene flow can and has occurred among the races.

Only two areas of any real disagreement exist between the traditional creationists and evolutionists. First, the creationists believe in Divine creation of the initial pair. The evolutionists, for the most part, believe in some sort of spontaneous generation. Second, the creationists believe that the races of men evolved (or developed as they prefer to say) over a few generations. The evolutionists believe that they evolved over tens of thousands, if not several hundreds of thousands, of years.

Both the traditional creationists and evolutionists ignore the fact that man can only invent falsehoods in science and religion. True science is nothing more than God's revelation through His work in nature. New discoveries in science may conflict with religious errors preached over the centuries.* With religious truths, however, they can never conflict. For both science and Scripture have the same Author.

Image of God

"And God created man [Adam] in his own image, in the image of God he created him. . . ."(Gen. 1:27). Adam had the physical nature of the Universe. He possessed life as found in other animals. But he was more. God had made Adam distinctly different. Like other races of men, Adam possessed reason, personality, and freewill. Unlike the other races of men, he was created in the image of God. He possessed special qualities of God lacking in other races. Adam was the first man that God made in His own image.

Pre-Adamic men were not created in the image of God—at least not in the sense that this phrase is used in Genesis. Pre-Adamic men had no closer union with their Creator than do their untutored descendants (Turanians, Negroes, Melanochroi, Khoisans, and Australians) have today.

Adam, however, was unique. God had made him as a special image of His own eternity. God made Adam immortal (this immortality Adam lost through sin). He was a creature, a species of man, with whom God could visit and have fellowship and communion (this unique fellowship with God, the Adamic race lost when Adam sinned). He possessed a spiritual quality lacking in others. This spiritual quality was directly related in

---

*A flat earth and a geocentric universe are the prime examples of religious error conflicting with science.

kinship to God. He had the ability to think God's thoughts in purity and holiness without corruption. Adam had the capacity to communion with God as no other race could. He could reach spiritual heights unattainable to the other species of men. God gave Adam a moral and spiritual nature that enabled him to understand his Creator, to commune with Him in this life, and to look forward to eternal bliss.

Among the Divine qualities identified by Campbell that God gave Adam was a conscience or moral sense. This conscience in the Adamic race differs entirely from that in the other species of men. In the other races of men, conscience is a perceptive faculty. It provides them with some idea of right and wrong, but it never causes them to feel as though they must do right except where doing right is expedient. When they do wrong, they seem to lack an inward accuser or judge. They seldom show remorse about their crimes or sins; they only have remorse about being caught. In Adamic man conscience provides moral guidance and protection from sinning. It is an innate part of his moral and spiritual constitution. His conscience convicts him of sin.* Conscience of Adamic man is entirely different from that of other men†

---

*This does not deny that many Aryans have dulled their conscience so much that they no longer feel its pricks. History is full of examples of Aryans with such a dulled conscience.

†Aryans who have destroyed their own conscience and their non-Aryan allies have often manipulated this conscience to the detriment of their fellow Aryans of conscience. The Aryans of conscience are manipulated to act against their best interest, even to sin, because of false guilt instilled upon their

Adam's unique privilege before God was conditioned by his obedience and responsibility to God. God had created Adam and the Adamic, Aryan, race to be his representative and steward on the Earth. God had delegated to Adam a share of His own authority. He made Adam a responsible being. The Divine purpose for the Adamic race was world dominion. (Because of sin, the Adamic race can now only achieve its Divine purpose by the intervention of Christ Jesus.)

"And Jehovah God formed man [Adam] of the dust of the ground, and breathed into his nostrils the breath of life; and man became a living soul." (Genesis 2:7) Thus, God breathed His spirit into Adam and made him a living soul. This, God did not do for the other species of men. This is what separates Adamic man from the other races. The other races do not possess the ever-living spirit of God as does Adamic man. Unlike other beings, he shared something in common with his Creator.

Location of Eden

According to the Scriptures, the Adamic race originated in Eden. Most people erroneously place Eden in the Middle East. The location of Eden is described in Genesis 2:8, 10-14. This description places it in Central Asia.

"And Jehovah God planted a garden eastward in Eden; and there he put man [Adam] whom he had

---

conscience by fellow Aryans and non-Aryans. A prime example is race. Aryans of conscience are made to feel guilty about crimes that they have not committed and are urged to breed themselves out of existence.

formed." (Genesis 2:8) The garden in Eden was eastward or "in the east" (Moffatt's translation) or "to the far east" (Ferrar Fenton's translation). If Moses were the author of Genesis as the fundamentalists claim, then he, being a highly educated man, would have been knowledgeable of the Mesopotamian region.* Would not he have said that Eden was in the land of Shinar or Mesopotamia if that is where it was? In Genesis 10:10, 11:2, 14:1, and 24:10, he calls this region Shinar or Mesopotamia. Moses identified Eden as being in the east because it was east of the area of which he had knowledge.

Also Sargon's Chronicle identifies Eden as being east of Mesopotamia. Thus, the inhabitants of Mesopotamia knew that they did not live where Eden was. Saint Ephraem's *Hymns to the True Paradise* and Cosmas Indicopleusters's *Christian Topography* place Eden at the western edge of the world's highest mountains. Hence, it was in the region of the Himalayan and adjacent mountains—although they may have thought of these mountains as being near the North Pole. They certainly did not place it in Mesopotamia.

According to the information given in Genesis 2:10-14, one river came out of Eden and divided into four. Because the Euphrates is mentioned as one of these rivers, most people assume that Eden was in Mesopotamia. Under this theory the Tigris is the

---

*If Genesis were written by various people who lived long after Moses as many modernists and liberal theologians claim, then these authors certainly would have been familiar with Mesopotamian region and would have referred to it by name rather than by a vague direction if that is where Eden were located.

Hiddekel. There is much dispute about the two rivers corresponding to Pison and Gihon. Some identify these two rivers with canals between the Euphrates and Tigris. The Karun and Kerkha Rivers have been identified as the other two rivers. Others identify them with various small rivers in Turkey. Some go as far as to identify them with the Indus, Ganges, and Nile. People who locate Eden in Mesopotamia generally locate it near Eridu (Abu Sharem).* This city was the home of Adapa, the Babylonian Adam.

The geography of Mesopotamia does not fit the description of Eden given in Genesis. Only two major rivers are in Mesopotamia: the Euphrates and Tigris. They merge rather than divide. Eden must be located elsewhere.

"Euphrates" in Hebrew is *perath* and means "a river of the east" (Strongs O.T. #6578). For centuries the "Pison" has been identified with the Indus or Ganges Rivers in India. (As noted above some who place Eden in Mesopotamia identify one of the rivers of Eden with one of these two rivers.) In the ancient records Havilah was equivalent to India. Because the Gihon was said to "compasseth the whole land of Ethiopia," some Biblical scholars identify the Gihon with the Nile. The word "cush" originates in northern India. Here the Hindu Cush mountains still bear that name. The Hiddekel is often identified as the Tigris. If the Tigris were also called the Hiddekel, it like the Euphrates was named for the original river in Eden. Probably this is why in Genesis 2:14 it is

---

*Another popular location for Eden is the Armenian Highlands at the headwaters of the Euphrates and Tigris.

referred to as the river that flows "toward the east of Assyria." This modifier would prevent confusing it with the river of the same name that flows within Assyria. Except for the Indus River, the rivers commonly thought of as flowing out of Eden do not fit the Biblical description of these rivers.

One place does resemble the description of Eden given in the Bible. That place is the Pamir Plateau in Central Asia between the Hindu Cush on the south and the Tien Shan mountains on the north. Four great rivers flow from this plateau. These are the Indus, Jaxartes (or Syr Darya), Oxus (or Amu Darya, also called Gihon), and Tarim. Corresponding to the Pison is the Kumar (or Chitral) branch of the Indus. The Jaxartes is the original Euphrates. The Tarim (that is its northern branch, the Kashgar River) flows to the east and is probably the Hiddekel. Most likely, the country of Havilah corresponds to the country of Darada toward Chachmises, which is noted for its riches.

The Pamir Plateau is different from what it was ten thousand years ago. A catastrophe has altered it. Then the plateau was lower and the climate much milder. Today the Pamir Plateau is uninhabited. It covers an area of about 180 by 180 miles and rises 15,000 feet above sea level. Too inhospitable to be inhabited, it is a blank and mysterious place. It is now the "roof of the world."

The Pamir Plateau matches the geographical description of Eden given in Genesis. It is the land in the east, and it has four great rivers flowing out of it.*

---

*See *The Origin of Race and Civilization* by Charles A. Weismen and *Tracing Our White Ancestors (White Roots)* by Frederick Haberman for further proof that the Pamir Plateau

The Serpent in the Garden of Eden

Many people generally think of the serpent in the Garden of Eden as a snake with four legs that could talk, perhaps as a result of some miracle. Such an erroneous concept has led some to argue a form of evolution: Snakes originally had four legs (or perhaps two if they stood upright as some believe), but with the Fall they changed into a legless creature. Others seeing this flaw argue that the serpent was a unique creature. Some claim that the snake was Satan himself.

The serpent of Genesis Three refers to pre-Adamic man, not to a reptile. In Genesis Three the word translated "serpent" is the Hebrew word *nâchâsh*, which is derived from *nâchash* (Strongs O.T. #5172). *Nâchash* means to whisper a (magic) spell or to prognosticate. It refers to enchantment in a subtle manner like a whisper. In Genesis Three, "serpent" is used as a descriptive name ("he is as sly as a snake") and does not refer to a reptile. It describes the personal characteristic of the person who deceived Eve (Genesis 3:13). In Genesis 3:1 the serpent is described as cunning (Moffatt, NKJV, St. Joseph), crafty (NASV, NEB), or clever (Smith)—"more than any beast of the field."

A snake is not thought of as cunning, crafty, or clever, especially more than any other animal. However, these terms do describe man. Hence, *nâchâsh* should not be thought of as a serpent, but as a human enchanter. A pre-Adamic man, under the control or influence of Satan, charmed and deceived Eve.

---

was the location of Eden.

Further evidence that "serpent" refers to a man and not a reptile is given in Genesis 3:15. In this verse God tells the serpent that He "will put enmity between thee [the serpent] and the woman, and between thy seed and her seed." That snakes would be adversaries of the Adamic race is absurd. That non-Adamic races would be has been proven by history.

This concept of a "serpent" describing a human is supported by the New Testament. In Matthew 23:33, Jesus calls the Pharisees serpents and offsprings of vipers.* Here "serpent" is the translation of *óphis* (Strongs N.T. #3789), which means "a snake, figuratively (as a type of sly cunning) an artful malicious person." This word is used in 2 Corinthians 11:3 where Paul writes that "the serpent beguiled Eve in his craftiness."

This man, who is called a serpent, who tempted Eve to sin was under the influence of Satan. Satan† was using him to destroy God's great creation, Adamic man. As a lesser being than Eve, the serpent appealed to Eve's animal nature. Next to Adamic man, he was God's most cunning and beautiful earthly creation. He seemed to have had more knowledge about the effects of eating the forbidden fruit of the "tree of knowledge of good and evil" than did Adam or Eve. His prediction that they, Adam and Eve, would know "good and evil" if they did eat the fruit proved true. However, his prediction that they would not die proved false. Although they did not

---

*Could he have been accusing the Jewish leaders of being a mongrel people, a hybrid of the Aryan race and another race?

†Ezekiel 28:12-19 and Isaiah 14:12-14 suggest that Satan was the real tempter in the Garden of Eden.

immediately die, their bodies began the aging process that would eventually lead to death.

When Did the Fall Occur?

How much time passes before Adam and Eve sinned is unknown. Some believed that their sin occurred within 48 hours of their creation. It probably occurred much later than this, for walking with Jehovah God in the cool of the day (Genesis 3:8) had become a habit or routine. Also, enough time had to pass to allow God to teach Adam the rudiments of civilization. (The purpose of Adam and the Aryan race is to glorify God by civilizing the pre-Adamic races of men and teaching them about their creator, Jehovah God.) However, that many years elapsed between Adam's creation and his fall is unlikely.

4
FROM THE FALL TO THE FLOOD

This Chapter attempts to shed some light on where Adam and Eve went after the fall and where Cain went when he was driven from the face of the earth. It also sheds some light on the activities of the Adamites as they interacted with the other races around them between the Fall and the Flood.

Did Death Occur Before Adam Sinned?

Did death occur before Adam sinned? Six-day creationists, for the most part, claim that death did not occur until after Adam sinned. If Adam's fall occurred within a few days of his creation, this belief presents little problem. Carnivorous animals just lived a few days without eating. However, if Adam's fall occurred several years after his creation, much needs to be explained away. Those who believe that life existed on Earth long before Adam's creation naturally believe that death occurred before Adam sinned.

To support the theory that death did not occur before Adam's fall, six-day creationists quote Romans 5:12-21, 1 Corinthians 15:21,22, Isaiah 11:6-9, and Genesis 3:20. Romans 5:12 and 1 Corinthians 15:21-22 state that Adam's sin brought about spiritual and physical death to man. Genesis 3:20 reads, ". . . Eve . . . was the mother of all living." Isaiah 11:6-9 describes God's picture of ideal conditions in the animal kingdom. Therefore, this is the way animals must have behaved before the fall because God saw that everything that He had made was good.

The six-day creationists in essence claim that all plant and animal life was immortal until Adam sinned. Using Genesis 1:30, they claim that no carnivorous animals lived before Adam sinned. All animals were herbivores.

When confronted with the obvious that as soon as an animal bites a plant, plant cells die, they counter with the argument that plant cells do die when eaten, but not the plant itself. (If plants did not die before the Fall, no plants that are today called annuals, i.e., plants that live for less than a year and then die, existed before the Fall. As God did not create these plants after the Fall, then they must have come into being via evolution.) They must also believe that animals scrupulously removed the microscopic insects and anthropoids and the one-cell amebas from the plants before eating them. They would have to have done so if death did not enter the world until Adam sinned. They must hold either this belief or the belief that these minute animals evolved after Adam sinned.

If carnivores and insectivores did not exist before the Fall, how could some plants avoid death? Without creatures to eat insects and herbivores, certainly some plants would have died of the onslaught of these plant eaters. The balance of nature would have been severely skewed against the plant kingdom.

Six-day creationists must explain away other problems. If no animals died before Adam's fall in sin, then the larger animals were very careful not to step on smaller animals, and all animals somehow managed to avoid life-threatening accidents. This seems incredulous. However, if animals were immortal as the six-day creationists claim or imply, then accidents present no problems. Animals would survive all accidents no matter how disastrous.

Further, if animals were immortal, animals eating animals present no problem. Being immortal, animals could have eaten each other, for no death would have been involved in being eaten. The eaten animal would merely exit the digestive tract alive and presumably whole. If not whole, then it presumably would immediately reconstitute itself once it was excreted. Such a possibility is incredulous and is not supported by reason, science, or, more importantly, the Scriptures.

Genesis 1:30 reads, "and to every beast of the earth, and to every bird of the heavens, and to everything that creepeth upon the earth, wherein there is life, I have given every green herb for food: and it was so." All animals, plant eaters and meat eaters, ultimately derive their substance and nourishment from plants. Animals that eat plants do so directly. Animals that eat animals do so indirectly. If this verse is read in the light of this fact, it no longer mandates the belief that all animals were initially created as herbivores.

To claim that Adam's sin caused death in animals creates a causal relationship that is extremely difficult to understand and explain. Adam's sin was a moral act. The transformation of a herbivore into a carnivore would be a structural change in a brute beast that had no moral nature. Where is the connection? The two are essentially and utterly unrelated.

If no carnivorous animals lived on Earth before the Fall, then God must have created them after the Fall or reengineered some animals after the Fall to convert them from herbivores to carnivores so that they could eat, digest, and thrive on flesh. Scriptural evidence that God created any new life forms after the Adamic race cannot be found. To the contrary carnivores are presented as part of the original creation week. According to Genesis 1:20-25, God made the animals "after their kind," i.e., herbivores descended from herbivores and carnivores descended from carnivores; carnivores did not descend from herbivores. (If they did, evolution is proved.) Also Exodus 20:11 states, "for in six days Jehovah made heaven and earth, the sea, and all that in them is. . . ." Hence, God made the carnivores during the creation week, not afterwards. If God reengineered herbivores to convert them to carnivores, then the theory of the theistic evolutionists is supported. The six-day creationists must resort to evolution to account for carnivores.

Whether or not animals died before the Fall is not stated in the Scriptures. The Genesis account only mentions death with reference to the Adamites. Adam was told that if he ate the forbidden fruit, then the day that he ate it he would surely die (Genesis 2:17). To extend this death penalty to the irrational animals is speculation. If Adam were to have some idea of what death meant, he would have needed some example of death around him. Moreover, reasons exist to believe that death in the animal realm was natural or usual before the Fall. No mention is made in the Bible of the sudden introduction of death or violence into the animal world.

Psalm 104 does suggest that death occurred before the Fall. It also suggests that animals ate meat before then. The activities of lions are reflected upon in Psalm 104:21 in light of God's regulation of night and day by means of the Sun. The predatory activity of lions is seen as perfectly natural as the rising of the Sun.

In conclusion, the most plausible and credible interpretation is that God created the Adamic species to be immortal. However, with Adam's sin, death entered the Aryan species, and it lost its immortality. Such is the proper understanding of Romans 5:12.* Before Adam's creation, animals and even non-Adamic man experienced death.

Furthermore, Adam may have eaten meat before the fall. The Scriptures clearly state that he was allowed to eat plant life (Genesis 1:30). He was only forbidden to eat fruit of a certain tree. However, no explicit prohibition against eating meat is stated. Although Genesis 9:3 does imply that such a prohibition may have existed, it does not emphatically state that such prohibition did exist.

Genesis 9:3 reads, "Every moving thing that liveth shall be food for you, as the green herb have I given you all." God had much earlier approved man taking the life of animals. In Genesis 4:4 Abel offered God the firstlings of his flock; God respected Abel and his offering. Furthermore, "Jehovah God made for Adam and for his wife coats of skin. . . ." (Genesis 3:21). God slew an animal to make clothes for Adam and Eve. Such action

---

*Some believe that if Adam and Eve had not sinned, they would have undergone a physical change that differed from dying that would have translated them into a higher condition. By sinning they forfeited this possibility. Because of sin they sank to the condition of the inferior animals and had to suffer corporal death.

would strongly suggest God's approval of slaying animals for their skins. If man killed animals for their skins, why not for their meat? If God approved the slaying of animals, why would He condemn eating the flesh thereof, especially when He would later state that eating meat was all right. Perhaps Genesis 9:3 is merely a reaffirmation of what man could eat.

Another indication that Adam may have eaten meat before his fall is that Jesus ate meat after his resurrection (Luke 24:42-43). If Jesus, the perfect man, the very Son of God, ate animal life in his resurrected body, does it not follow that man will, or at least may, eat meat in his resurrected body? If animals are food for the resurrected, could they not have also been food before Adam's fall without violation to God's good creation? Furthermore, if Jesus, who is, according to Trinitarian doctrine, God himself, did take the lives of animals and eat them, can such an act be bad, a violation of God's good creation?

Where Did Adam Go When Driven from Eden?

According to Genesis 3:24, Adam went east when he left Eden. If Eden were located where the Pamir Plateau is now, east of the Pamir Plateau is the Tarim Basin of Eastern Turkestan.* This region fits the description of the Flood.

The Tarim Basin was the primary homeland of the Adamic race until God caused all the inhabitants thereof, except Noah and his family, to drown in the Flood.

---

*See Appendix 2 for a description of the Tarim Basin.

From the Tarim Basin the Adamites came forth to build the great civilizations of the world. Many anthropologists and historians place the origin of man's beginning in Central Asia. Central Asia is also the origin of the Aryan race.

Rise of the Cainites

After leaving Eden, Eve bore two sons, Cain and Abel. Cain became a farmer while Abel became a herdsman.

Cain murdered his brother because God accepted Abel's gift while rejecting his. God confronted Cain about his sinful deed. Part of his punishment was banishment from the fertile plains where he lived to Nod. Nod appeared to have been an area not suitable for agriculture. God told Cain, "when thou tillest the ground, it shall not henceforth yield unto thee its strength" (Genesis 4:12a). He would be unable to sustain himself by farming as he had in the past. He would become a herdsman, wandering from one place to another until he founded a city for his son, Enoch, and began building an empire.

When Cain was driven "from the face of the earth," he was driven eastward into the land of Nod, which was in what is now western China. There he took a wife from among the native people, who were Turanians, probably Turks.

Cain gained predominance over the aboriginal people of Nod. When Cain arrived in Nod, he found the Turanians living in the state of a Paleolithic culture. He brought them the Neolithic culture. Thus, Cain's arrival among the Turks of Eastern Turkestan commenced the Neolithic Age. He introduced these Turks to the arts of domesticating animals and plants, making ceramic pottery, and constructing walled cities. He may have introduced them to the worship of the dragon. With his superior knowledge he became their leader.

He used the labor of his subjects to erect a city in honor of his son Enoch (Genesis 4:17)[*] The ancient city of Khara-khota (or perhaps more correctly, the city that preceded this city at this location) in the Gobi Desert is most likely the city Cain built for Enoch. From this city he established the ancient Uighur Empire[†] that stretched from the Pacific Ocean and Farther India into Europe.[#]

The Uighur Empire of Cain had a high level of civilization and culture. They knew writing, mining, textiles, mathematics, astrology, agriculture, and other sciences. They were also skillful artists. The Uighur

---

[*]Sayce believed that the city built by Cain for Enoch may have been the Babylonian City of Unuk or Erech. Khara-khota is more likely the city that Cain build for Enoch.

[†]Shambhala (or Xembala) may be another name for the Uighur Empire. Shambhala was described as an island surrounded by a large sea in Central Asia. It was probably located in the Gobi Desert. This civilization vanished along with the inland sea. Perhaps it was destroyed during the Flood.

[#]Supporters of the theory that a continent named Mu once existed where the Pacific Ocean now exists claim that the Uighur Empire was the principal colonial empire of Mu. A more likely explanation is that the Uighur Emigre was founded by Cain.

civilization may have been the origin of the Babylonian culture.*

About 8000 B.C., or shortly thereafter, he led an army out of western China and marched northward and then westward across Central Asia (present-day Kazan and Western Turkestan) to the region south of the Caspian Sea. In his trek westward his band grew by conquest and consent. Most of the people brought under his sway were of the Turanian race. Later Aryans came under his rule. Thus, the Cain's Uighur Empire, which may have been little more than a loose confederation, may have stretched from the Aral and Caspian Seas on the west well into the Gobi Desert, and perhaps as far as the East China Sea, on the east, and from the Kirgiz Steppe and Altai Mountains on the north into Tibet on the south and perhaps even into Farther India at its greatest extent.

The Cainites built cities and established a civilization in what is now the Kara Kum Desert of Turkmenistan. The cities were laid out according to a plan. There were residential quarters and artisans' quarters as well as religious edifices. This kingdom and civilization may have been founded by Cain's grandson Irad.

Evidence exists that Cainites migrated to India. People called the Melanides came to India from the region of Lop Nor of the Tarim Basin. They had arrived in India before 3500 B.C. These people, called the Naachals by the Dravidians, brought the native Dravidians knowledge of the ten-digit numerical system. Before their

---

*Merodach or Marduk, Babylonian sun-god and patron-god of Babylon, may be the deification of Cain.

departure to India, the Melanides had close ties with the Cainites of the Gobi Desert.*

Many of the amenities of civilization are credited to the Cainites. Cain and Enoch were the founders of the first city (Genesis 4:17). Jubal was the originator of the musical arts (Genesis 4:21), and Tubal-cain, working in metals (Genesis 4:22).

Tubal-cain was "an instructor of every artificer in brass and iron" (Genesis 4:22). He was perhaps deified as Daedalus, the Cretan god who was the father of all artificers and inventors. He is also credited with being the father of witchcraft and sorcery.

The Chinese civilization was primarily a descendant of the Cainite civilization. It was, however, modified from time to time by contact with western Aryans.

Pre-Flood Migration of Aryans

God created the Aryans about 8100 B.C. on the Pamir Plateau. By 8000 B.C. they migrated eastward into the Tarim Basin where they later encountered Turks, who lived in the eastern part of the basin.

Just before 8000 B.C. Turks came out of western Tibet and down into the Tarim Basin. Soon afterwards the Neolithic Age appeared in Eastern Turkestan. Cain had brought the Neolithic culture with him when he was banished to the land of Nod, which the Turks inhabited. From here the Turks and later Aryans who had left the Tarim Basin spread this culture across Eurasia.

---

*Such contact is evidence that Cainites, Aryans, and even pre-Adamic man moved into and out of the Tarim Basin, the land of Noah, before the Flood.

Not long afterwards Cain began establishing his empire. Aryans began commingling with the Cainite Turks. Although many intermarried with the Turks, many also retained their racial integrity.

About 7800 B.C. several tribes of Aryans left the Tarim Basin. Part of them journeyed to the Altai Mountains and became the progenitors of the Finns, and part journeyed to Western Turkestan and became the progenitors of the Pre-Sumerians and Sumerians.

The Finns spread across the Altai Mountains and displaced the Turanians who were living there. They gradually crossed the mountains and settled along the Yenisey, Obi, and Irtysh Rivers, from their headwaters to just north of the Sayan and Altai Mountains. Here they became known as the Tshcudes or Chudes.

About 7800 B.C. bands of Turks came out of central Tibet and invaded the foothills of the Hindu Kush, the Pamirs, and the valleys of the upper Amu Darya. Their arrival forced the Celtic inhabitants of these highlands down the mountains into Western Turkestan. These Celts collided with Aryans in the valleys and caused them to migrate.

While Turks were pushing the Celts out of the mountains, other Turks were forcing Nordics of the Tarim Basin to flee across the Tien Shan into Western Turkestan south and southeast of Lake Balkhash where they settled (c. 7700 B.C.). (This region became known as Geté.) Here they stayed for about a thousand years. During this time they split into five nations: Suebians (Suebi), Cimmerians, Getae (Goths), Massagetae, and Sakae.

The Turks followed the Nordics across the mountains, but instead of pursuing them, the Turks veered eastward into Western Turkestan. This maneuver caused many of the Celts who had previously been driven from the mountains to go west. Skirting along the southern shores of the Caspian Sea, these Celts crossed the Caucasus Mountains and traveled through Ukraine to central Europe. They migrated up the Danube valley and gradually spread over central and northern Europe from the Black Sea to the Atlantic and north to the Baltic plains, Scandinavia, and British Isles. They became known as the Paleo-Celts. Other Celts remained in the Pamirs surrounded by Turks.

The Paleo-Celts introduced the Maglemosean and shell-mound cultures into northwestern Europe. They also brought the lake-dwelling culture to the Alps and surrounding areas. A Paleo-Celtic people known as the Furfooz-Grenelle people had reached the North Sea by 7500 B.C. As the Paleo-Celts, and later Mediterraneans, spread across Europe, they displaced the earlier Melanochroi.

Some of these Paleo-Celts may have settled the shores of northern Africa as evidenced by the blond-haired, blue-eyed people reported by the ancients scattered throughout northern Africa. They may have been the ancestors, or one of the Aryan ancestors, of the fair-skinned, blue-eyed, blond Libyans depicted on ancient Egyptian monuments. (Other ancestors of these people may have been the Mediterranean Libyans, who were the primary ancestors of the Southern Mediterranean Aryans, and Nordic Cimmerians, who settled in Libya after 1500 B.C.)

A band of these Aryans crossed into the Iranian Plateau about 7600 B.C. near the present-day city of Herat. Within a few centuries they had driven many of the Melanochroi of the Iranian Plateau across the Zagros Mountains into the Lower Mesopotamia or into the mountain valleys of Afghanistan. These Aryans followed the Melanochroi across the Zagros and pushed them westward toward the Mediterranean and Africa and southward toward Arabia. At Sousa in Elam, the Aryans established a colony and became known as Pre-Sumerians. They introduced the Neolithic culture into the Middle East.

From Sousa the Pre-Sumerians extended their control up Mesopotamia until they controlled the Fertile Crescent. Then they extended their control into Anatolia (Asia Minor) and Palestine. Among the nations descended from the Pre-Sumerians were the Assyrians, Elamites,* Palestinians, Leleges, Hyksos (Kheta), Hurrians, Gutians, Lullubians, and Kassites.

Mediterranean Aryans had either accompanied the Pre-Sumerian Aryans to the Middle East or arrived shortly after these people had taken control of this land. Some of them settled in Anatolia while others settled in the western part of the Fertile Crescent to northern Arabia and Lower Egypt. Some of these Mediterraneans, the ancestors of the Pelasgians, joined the Pre-Sumerians as they extended their control over Anatolia. Others, the

---

*There were two races of Elamites: the Aryan Pre-Sumerians and the Melanochroi who lived in Elam before the Pre-Sumerians arrived and after the Pre-Sumerians left.

ancestors of the Libyans,[†] Iberians, and Ligurians, spread across North Africa.

About 7500 B.C. the Mediterranean Pelasgians crossed into Europe and introduced the Neolithic culture in the Balkans. They crossed the Aegean Sea and gradually spread over much of southern and eastern Europe. The Mediterranean Ligurians crossed the Mediterranean into Italy about 7000 B.C. By 6500 B.C. they had migrated into southeastern France and Germany. Some even reached Scandinavia. While the Ligurians and Pelasgians were moving northward, the Iberians had entered the Iberian Peninsula from North Africa and were migrating across western France. As early as 6000 B.C. Iberians from the Iberian Peninsula had passed through Gaul and crossed into Britain.[†] Continuously pressed by the Paleo-Kelts, they had moved up the Rhone valley into western France by 6000 B.C. with their Neolithic culture and then into England. Over the centuries various Mediterranean people moved northward from the northern shores of the Mediterranean Sea. When they collided with the Celts, they frequently pushed the Celts northward and westward. However, more often than not, the Mediterraneans and Celts peacefully intermingled and intermarried.

While the Mediterranean Pelasgians were settling the Balkans, the Mediterranean Libyans were settling in Lower Egypt. Their arrival drove many of the

---

*These Libyans were the primary progenitors of the Riff, Kabyle, and related Berbers (Southern Mediterraneans) along the northern part of the Maghreb.

†These Iberians were known as the Silurians.

Melanochroic Egyptians up the Nile into Upper Egypt. Some time after 6000 B.C. the Eastern-Hamites came down the Nile and drove out many of these Mediterraneans, most of whom fled to Crete.* Here they later established the Cretan culture, which later spread to Greece.

Shortly after the arrival of the Pre-Sumerians in the Middle East another Aryan people called the Artaei entered the Iranian Plateau and settled in Fars Province of Iran. These people were of the Iranian racial type and the progenitors of the Persians proper. Iranians continued to enter Iran over the next several millennia.

The next noticeable Aryan invasion of the Middle East occurred about 3500 B.C. These invaders were the Sumerians. (The Aryan Hittites had driven them from Western Turkestan.) They entered the in Lower Mesopotamia about 3500 B.C. and established the Sumerian civilization. Eridu was the first city that they founded. Next they founded Nippur in the northwest. Babylon was a colony of Eridu while Ur was a colony of Nippur. Some of these cities may have been built on settlements of Pre-Sumerians, who in turn may have taken over sites that the Melanochroi had established earlier.

---

*This was one of many contests between the Aryans, primarily Mediterraneans, and Melanochroi, primary Egyptians but often Eastern-Hamites, for supremacy of Lower Egypt. (Since their arrival, the Egyptians have held Upper Egypt although they were frequently ruled by Mediterraneans, Eastern-Hamites, and other people.) In the end the Egyptians won.

While the Sumerians (and at times Pre-Sumerians) maintained control of Mesopotamia, trade between the Sumerians and Turks in Turkestan was maintained. Keeping the caravan routes open across Iran forced continuous emigration of Melanochroi into India.

About 3300 B.C. the Flood occurred. Not long afterwards Noah's descendants begin arriving in the Middle East.

5
THE FLOOD

Was the Flood universal or local? If it were local, where did it occur? The information provided by the Bible and confirmed by archeology, biology, and geology testifies against a universal flood. Contrary to the claims of the traditional creationists, the Bible reveals that all people on Earth were not destroyed during the Flood.

Use of the Word "All"

Supporters of the universal flood theory quote Genesis 7:19-24, which says that the earth was covered and all flesh died except those in the Ark. They take a literal reading of this passage.

However, Luke 2:1 reads, "that all the world should be taxed" (KJV). This verse means that all the world under Roman rule should be taxed, as much as the Romans wished that they could have taxed the entire planet. Few would argue that "all the world" in this verse means the entire planet.

Genesis 41:57 reads, "all countries came into Egypt to buy grain." This verse is referring to countries in Egypt's sphere of influence. It should not be interpreted to mean that people from America came to Egypt for grain.

Exodus 9:6 states that "all the cattle of Egypt died." Exodus 9:19-22 refers to the cattle of Pharaoh and the Egyptians in such a way that not all of these cattle did die during the previous plague, but that they would suffer from the next plague. Here "all" obviously means a large number but not every last one.

1 Kings 10:24 states that "and all the earth sought the presence of Solomon, to hear his wisdom. . . ." Here "all the earth" means the Middle East. It could not possibly have included America or Australia. These two continents were unknown at this time.

As the above passages clearly show, universal terms, such as "all," need not always be understood in the strictly literal sense. Such words are often used as hyperboles, i.e., as an exaggeration to emphasize the largeness of the number. Thus, in Genesis 7:19 "all" and "whole" may not be literal. Some passages do occur in which "all" means all in the sense of every last one; the context tells if such a reading is intended.

Use of the Word "Earth"

Universalists claim that the word "earth" in Genesis Seven means the whole planet. What is really meant in Genesis Seven by the word "earth" is that part of the Earth that Noah inhabited, the Flood destroyed. The Hebrew word *'erets* is translated in the King James Version as "earth" in Genesis Seven and in Genesis 4:14 where Cain said, "Behold thou hast driven me out this day from the face of the earth." Cain was driven from the land of his parents, not from the planet Earth (or else the land of Nod was on another planet, which no one really believes except perhaps some of the "God was an astronaut" crowd). So it was with the Flood: It covered the land inhabited by Noah, not the entire planet. This is the way these passages should be understood if they are to be understood consistently.

'Erets (Strong #776) comes from the root "to be firm." Not only does it mean the entire terrestrial earth, it also can mean its component parts: land, country, ground, or soil. It is frequently translated as such in other passages of the Bible. In Genesis 4:14 Fenton, Amplified Bible, Lamsa, Berkeley, and JPSA translate 'erets as "this land." Moffatt translates it as "country." RSV and NEB translate it as "ground." In Genesis Seven 'erets can correctly be translated "ground" or "land." Thus, the Flood destroyed the land of Noah.

The interpretation of the description of the Noahic Flood in Genesis should be that the Flood killed all the people, except the eight in the Ark, in the land of Noah. That the Flood killed every human on the planet except those in the Ark is an incorrect interpretation.

Races of Men Support a Local Flood

Seldom is a creationist found who does not proclaim the Flood of Noah's time to be worldwide. A worldwide flood presents obvious problems about the origin of the races of men. The creationists who believe in a universal flood believe that all the people of the world were destroyed except Noah, his sons, and their wives. Thus, they argue that all the races of men are descended from Noah through his sons. Noah, therefore, is the origin and common ancestor of all the races of men. They are forced to place the development (evolution) of the races after the Flood, which many claim occurred about 2348 B.C. (Usher's chronology). However, they do not explain just how one racial family could have produced the numerous racial types that now exist without resorting to evolutionist arguments. They cannot provide such explanation without doing violence to the Scriptures (like beget like)* and the laws of genetics (like beget like).

In an attempt to avoid some of these problems, some of these creationists claim that Noah's family was multiracial. However, the Bible refutes this claim. It describes Noah and his family as being of one race. In Genesis 6:9, Noah is described as "perfect in his generation." The word "generation" is the Hebrew word *tôledâh*, which means "descent" (Strong's O. T. #8435). Thus, Noah was perfect in his descent from Adam. No one in his lineage had mixed with another race. Therefore, if all the races of men descended from Noah, then some form of accelerated evolution must have occurred sometime after the Flood. No evidence exists in the Scriptures or science that such accelerated evolution occurred.

A closely related argument used by supporters of the theory that all the races of men descended from Noah is the claim that his sons and daughters-in-law carried all the genes of the modern races. Noah and his family were all of the same race, for God had destroyed all the people who had committed the sin of miscegenation. Yet all the races of men are supposed to have descended from them. Do like beget unlike? If this theory were true, Negroes should be carrying all the genes of Turanians and Aryans. They should be producing Turanians and Aryans today. The races of men are not like modern breeds of domestic animals that have been formed by authoritarian breeding. An authoritarian breeder has not formed the races of

---

*Chapter 1 of Genesis uses the phrase "after his kind." Chapter 11 of Leviticus also uses this or similar phrase to refer to the immutability of species.

men. Unlike domestic breeds, they have not been formed by an authoritarian breeder selecting the parents to be bred and destroying undesirable offspring. Such a breeding program would have to occur if the races of men were to descend from Noah. (Then such a program could only succeed if Noah's sons and daughters-in-law carried all the genes necessary to make all the races of men, which is highly unlikely.) Otherwise, Noah's descendants would have continued to interbreed, and no racial distinctions would have occurred.*

The universalists resort to evolutionist arguments to explain the origin of races. Mutations occurring in isolated groups, claim the universalists, brought about the races of men. Mutations occurring in isolated groups, claim the evolutionists, brought about the races of men. On the other hand, creationists, and most universalists are creationists, when arguing against evolution claim that mutations do not lead to new species. At best, mutations are neutral. Most mutations are harmful or degrade the animal. However, if mutation brought about the races of men, then this argument has been disproved. Negroes do have a definite advantage over the Aryans in the environment of Central Africa. If mutation formed the Negroes, then the mutations were to his benefit. Thus,

---

*If Noah's family possessed all the genes of all the races of man, few Black people would be found in the world today. Blacks, as well as most other people, prefer lighter skin to darker skin. If natural selection were at work in forming the races, the darker skin people would try to mate with lighter skin people. They would have adopted an eugenics program similar to that of the mulattoes in the United States, Brazil, and elsewhere, to bred lighter colored offspring.

mutations can be beneficial, and the creationists have lost an argument against evolution. The universalists try to have their cake and eat it too, to use an old but appropriate cliche. Like the evolutionists, they claim that the species or races of men evolved from a common prototype ancestor. Yet they then claim that man did not evolve from an earlier ancestor. They cannot have it both ways. Evolution is either true or false. The only apparent difference between the universalists and the evolutionists is that the universalists argue that evolution occurs within a few generations* while the evolutionists argue that evolution occurs over hundreds or thousands of generations.

If Noah's descendants developed into the various races of men within a few generations after the Flood, then evolution is proved. No reason remains to disbelieve that evolution occurred over millions of years if evolution occurred over a few generations. If the traditional creationists are going to do the impossible with genetics, they should not complain when evolutionists do the same thing. Evolution is evolution whether the creationists or the evolutionists use it. If a reptile could not change into a mammal, then a group of White people could not change into Chinese, Negroes, etc., especially when only a few generations are allowed for this change to occur.

---

*Rapid evolution would explain the absence of the "missing link."

The other races of men where not destroyed by the Flood.* ". . . where there is no law, there is no transgression." Not knowing God's law, they were not held accountable. A cave painting, dating about 5,000 B.C., in South Africa shows that the Khoisan race has existed for at least 7,000 years.† The races of man that existed before the Flood existed after the Flood.

According to Genesis 6:4, "the Nephilim were in the earth in those days" before the Flood. When the spies reported to Moses about their findings in Canaan, they said, ". . . We saw the Nephilim, the sons of Anak, who came of the Nephilim . . ." (Numbers 13:33). The Nephilim lived before the Flood. They were still living around 1490 B.C. when the Israelite spies saw them. If the Flood destroyed all men except Noah and his sons and their wives, how could the Nephilim still exist in the time of Moses?# Did God destroy them just to recreate

---

*Actually not all Aryans were destroyed by the Flood. Only Aryans in and around the Tarim Basin were destroyed. Aryans living in Europe were hardly touched by the Flood.

†Why would God create a race of man, destroy it during the Flood, and recreate it afterwards?

#Many believe that God destroyed mankind in the Flood because of illicit sex between angels and the daughters of man. They claim that the Nephilim were the prodigy of this illicit sex. If the Nephilim were the product of these angels and the daughters of man, how could the Nephilim still be alive in the days of Moses? Had not God sent the Flood to destroy them? Did the fallen angels return after the Flood and impregnate earthly women and thereby defeat God's purpose for sending the Flood? Surely not.

them a few years later or did they evolve from one of Noah's sons?

The historical and archaeological evidence verifies the permanence of the races. The various racial types that exist today existed when the descendants of Noah settled in their respective territories. If the historical and archaeological evidence is rejected, then an unprecedented racial evolution must be accepted.

In summary, the races of men argue against a universal flood. Noah and his family were White. If like beget like as both the Bible and science claim, then Noah's descendants would have been white, not black, brown, or yellow. If other races of man descended from Noah, then evolution is proved.* Because they did not evolve from Noah, then they must have survived the Flood.

Animal Life Supports a Local Flood

Further evidence that universalists are evolutionists is found in how they define "kind." Some universalists prefer to say that Noah took pairs of each "kind" of animal instead of pairs of each "species" of animal. They prefer "kind" to "species" because it obfuscates their

---

* Some of the people who champion the doctrine of the universal flood attempt to explain away the several races of men by claiming that the "beast of the earth" refers to members of the other races of men. 1 Peter 3:20 says that only eight souls were saved from the Flood. If the "beast of the earth" were men, they were men without souls. 2 Peter 2:5 says that only Noah and seven others were saved from the Flood. These verses do imply that the "beast of the earth" does not refer to man.

theory of evolution. A "kind" is basically a prototype. For example, Noah did not take a pair of horses, a pair of zebras, a pair of quaggas onto the Ark. He took a horse-type animal, i.e., an Equus type of animal from which the modern-day horse, zebra, and quagga evolved. The horse, quagga, and zebra have a common ancestor. Not only does March, who is a universalist, believes this is true, he also believes that the Arctic fox, gray fox, red fox, wolf, dog, coyote, jackal, and hyena descended from the interbreeding of a fox-like creature, a dog-like creature, and a hyena-like creature. Noah, his wife, sons, and daughters-in-law apparently were not Aryans, Negroes, Turanians, or Melanochroi, but were proto-humanoids from whom the species of men have evolved. Such evolutionary descent the universalists present to prove evolution wrong! These universalists agree with the evolutionists that the various species within a family or genus of animals evolved from one or perhaps a few prototypes or proto-kinds. The evolutionists carry this process back further in their claims that this family prototype evolved from one or more order prototypes; and these order prototypes, from class prototypes and so on. The disagreement between universalists and evolutionists is not one of principle but one of degree. Both believe that like naturally beget unlike.

However, the Bible does not suggest that God created any new species (or kind) or recreated any old species after the Flood. If He planned to create, and especially to recreate, species, the Ark was not needed to preserve animals through the Flood.

The distribution of animal life argues against a universal flood. Edentates, which are slow-moving, nearly toothless animals like sloths, armadillos, and anteaters, are found in the jungles of South America. How could these animals have traveled from the Middle East to South America? Marsupials, which are poached animals like kangaroos and opossums, are found only in Australia and America. If they originated in the Middle East, why are none found in Europe, Asia, or Africa?

Creationists who support the local flood theory answer these questions by claiming God specifically created these animals for the zoological niches in which they are found. For the most part these animals have always been where they are now found.

The universalists claim that these animals like all the other animals found throughout the world migrated from a single point in the Middle East where the Ark landed to where they are today.* Again the universalists find themselves supporting the evolutionists. Both the universalists and evolutionists claim that animals migrated from distant places. In the case of Australia, both claim that the migration of marsupials was primarily across land bridges. The only real differences between the two schools are the rate of the migration and the rate and degree of evolution. The evolutionists claim that the migration occurred over thousands, perhaps, millions of years while the universalists claim that it occurred over a few decades. Whitcomb and Morris and other universalists essentially resort to evolutionist

---

* Supporters of the local flood theory do not deny that migrations of some species have occurred. They, however, believe such migrations are the exception instead of the rule. One should only claim that a species has migrated from one area to another when there is physical evidence to support that claim.

explanations to explain the presence of marsupials in Australia. Is not the explanation of special creation for that zoological niche simpler and more scripturally sound?

Some universalists imply that supporters of the local flood theory are either hypocrites or inconsistent when they appeal to the "evolutionary timescale" as evidence against a universal flood. By "evolutionary timescale" presumably the standard geological time frame of strata and the age of fossils found therein is meant.* Supporting the old-age Earth position does not necessitate supporting evolution. In fact, if the universalists are correct, evolution does not need millions upon millions of years to occur. It needs only a few generations.†

The frozen mammoths in Siberia argue against a universal flood. Enormous numbers, upwards of 5,000,000, of mammoths were frozen and buried wholly with flesh and hair intact. Unless the Flood occurred the way Patten hypothesizes, and most universalists reject his hypothesis, the Flood could not have left these remains.

---

*According to geological ageing scheme, the more advance the fossilized life-form found in the strata, the younger the strata. This principle is consistent with Genesis. Genesis describes God creating simpler life-forms before He created advanced life-forms.

†As this book shows over and over again, the disagreement that universalists have with evolutionists is not one of principle, but one of degree and especially of rate. The evolutionists believe that hundreds, thousands, or millions of years are required for one kind of animal to evolve into another while the universalists believe that such evolution occurs over a few generations.

If the Earth enjoyed a uniform subtropical climate from pole to pole just before the Flood as most universalists claim, how could they have frozen? No freezing temperatures existed when the Flood began. A flood violent enough to create all the fossil-bearing sedimentary strata would have been violent enough to keep water from freezing as well as keeping these animals from freezing. To freeze these mammoths intact would require a rapid drop in temperature; the temperature must have rapidly dropped to below $-150°$ Fahrenheit. Obviously these fossils were created by a catastrophe and a large scale catastrophe at that. However, this catastrophe could not have been the Flood unless Patten's hypothesis is correct.

Further, that such herds of mammoth could have been frozen after a recent global flood is highly questionable. How could such vast herds have come about within a few generations after the Flood? The mammoths may have survived predators, but many small species that are found fossilized in vast numbers along with the mammoths would have been prime food for many predators.

If the Flood were universal, how could the pairs of herbivores avoid the pairs of carnivores and survive long enough to reproduce? The carnivores, or at least the non-fishing ones, would have had nothing to eat but the animals that came off the Ark. Either they ate some of the herbivores to extinction, or they starved themselves to extinction.

The diversity of marine life argues against a universal flood. The salinity of the oceans would have been greatly altered. The tremendous amount of rain and erupting groundwater (much of this groundwater would have been freshwater) would have diluted the ocean. The resulting drop in salinity would have destroyed many of today's species of marine life and species that feed on them. Likewise, with many of today's freshwater species, they could not survive a rise in salinity. Freshwater would have become salted as the ocean waters rose to cover the land and thus mixing with the waters of rivers and lakes. Because many of today's species of fishes could not survive a rapid change in salinity, they must have evolved after the Flood if the Flood were universal.

In summary, the distribution of edentates, marsupials, and other animals and the diversity of marine life testify against a universal flood. Without resorting to evolutionary principles, the animal kingdom in general proves that the Flood was not universal. To prove that the Flood was universal requires evolution.

Plant Life Support to a Local Flood

Quoting Genesis 8:22, which reads, "While the earth remaineth, seedtime and harvest, and cold and heat, and summer and winter, and day and night shall not cease" and Genesis 9:20-21, which describes Noah's experience with wine, the universalists claim that the climate differed after the Flood from the climate before the Flood. Before the Flood a watery canopy caused the climate of the planet to be tropical or subtropical from pole to pole. After the Flood, seasons (Genesis 8:22) began, and Noah discovered fermented grape juice.

Noah's discovery of wine, fermented grape juice, argues more for a local flood than a global flood. Grape juice will ferment under tropical conditions. Therefore, grapes must have been new to Noah. Grapes did not grow in the region from which Noah came. However, they did grow in the region to which Noah went after the Flood.

If evolution is false, the wide variety of plants argues against a change in seasons caused by the Flood. Only a few plants that grow in the tropics or subtropics will grow in temperate climates, and even fewer will survive in the arctic climate. Vice versa many plants that thrive in temperate and arctic climates will not survive in tropical or subtropical climates. Furthermore, if the canopy theory is correct, altitude would not serve as a domain for cold loving plants for two reasons. First the higher mountains were not formed until the Flood catastrophe. Second the canopy would have caused the ground level temperature to be nearly the same over the face of the Earth, so uniform that little horizontal or vertical wind would have existed. If a significant global climate change occurred as a result of the Flood, as many universalists claim, then evolution is proved—not gradual evolution over millions of years that evolutionists claim, but some unheard of and unscriptural evolution over a few decades. Selective breeding does not solve the problem. Selective breeding does not bring about new families and orders. Anyway, why would Noah or his descendants want to breed weeds through selective breeding. The vast varieties of plants and the wide range of climates in which they live argue against a global Flood.

The canopy theory claims that the Earth was watered by a mist, i.e., heavy dew and possibly fogs, but not by rain, for rain did not fall until the Flood. If true, then much of the Earth must have been arid and semiarid or else essentially swampy. Dew and fog do not provide much water for plants. Under the canopy theory most of pre-Flood Earth was either warm, humid, swampy or warm, dry, semiarid or arid. Many plants that exist today cannot long survive under either of these types of climates. Therefore, these plants must have evolved after the Flood because the Scriptures contain no evidence of God creating new plants after the Flood.

If the pre-flood climate were subtropical from pole to pole as the canopy theory claims, then many plants and animals that exist today would not have existed before the Flood. The fossil remains of subtropical plants and animals found in the higher latitudes can be more easily explained by a shift in the poles perhaps caused by an astral catastrophe without a global subtropical climate. If pre-Flood Earth had arctic and temperate climate zones like Earth today, the canopy theory is disproved;* and the evolution of plants is not necessary.

Some long-lived plants, such as the bristle cone pine, provide additional evidence for a local flood. Some bristle cone pines are more than 6850 years old. Some are reported to be more than seven thousand years old. These pines lived before and after the flood. If a cataclysmic global flood changed the face of the Earth, then surely bristle cone pines that were growing before the Flood would have been destroyed. The existence of these trees disproves the occurrence of a universal flood several thousand years ago.

Like the animal kingdom, the plant kingdom testifies against a universal flood. The story of Noah and grapes

---

*Also, Genesis 1:16 talks about the Moon and stars. How could these be visible through a canopy of thick, unbroken layers of clouds? The simple answer is the canopy theory is false.

and the diversity of plant life proves that the Flood was local. When they use the plant kingdom to support their theory, the universalists must resort to evolution.

The Rainbow Covenant Supports a Local Flood

The covenant that God made with Noah and symbolized with the rainbow suggests that the Flood was not universal. He said, ". . . I establish my covenant with you, and with your seed after you; and with every living creature that is with you, the birds, the cattle, and every beast of the earth with you; of all that go out of the ark, even every beast of the earth" (Genesis 9:9, 10). Here God established His covenant with every beast that came out of the Ark and *"every beast of the earth."* The covenant was made with two different groups of beasts: those that were on the Ark and those that were not. "Every beast of the earth" refers to beasts not on the Ark, the beast remaining on the Earth that the Flood did not drown. If the Flood failed to destroy all animals outside the Ark, it could not have been universal.

Geology Supports a Local Flood

Genesis 8:1, which reads, ". . . God made a wind to pass over the earth, and the waters assuaged," supports the concept of a local flood. What is being described is the process of evaporation of a large body of water coupled with a gradual draining by outlets. Such an expression is completely inapplicable to the surface of the whole planet. Thus, the geological evidence argues against a universal flood.*

Coral reefs argue against a global flood. Coral reefs are structures that are built up slowly. Slow growth rates would be incompatible with reef formation during a brief period of the Flood year. Reefs generally grow only a few centimeters per year under ideal conditions.

Advocates of a global flood claim that the fossil reefs were antediluvian reefs that were eroded and redeposited during the Flood. They claim that enough time has elapsed since the Flood to allow the formation of the currently existing reefs. However, this position is untenable.

Could a reef that is almost 1000 feet thick and several miles in diameter be a redeposited antediluvian reef? Could any kind of flood dislodge and transport such a large structure without smashing it to pieces? Hardly. Yet the global flood cataclysmic theory demands such action, for all ancient fossil-containing rock is, according to this theory, the result of a global flood.

Furthermore, in the Midwest these gigantic reefs lie on top of other carbonate rocks, which in turn lie on top of sandstone that is 300 feet thick. These reefs would have had either to remain suspended while the carbonate rocks and sandstone were deposited, or else to be transported to and deposited on top of these rocks by a force powerful enough to move these gigantic reefs but gentle enough not to disturb the sediment, which would not have had enough time to solidify within a few

---

*For a more detailed discussion of the geological record disproving a universal Flood, see *Christianity & the Age of the Earth* by Davis A. Young.

weeks or months of continuous violent rushing water. A flood powerful enough to move these reefs would certainly have disturbed the sediment. Moreover, could a flood violent enough to keep such a gigantic reef suspended allow material that was of a much finer grain and of a lower density to be deposited under it? Floods generally deposit larger objects before they deposit smaller ones. Smaller objects tend to remain suspended longer.

Another piece of evidence that these reefs were not redeposited is that none are upside down. If a violent flood had transported these reefs, surely at least one of them would have been deposited upside down. All the evidence shows that these reefs grow in place over an already deposited carbonate sediment.

Reefs grow only in lightly agitated warm water. They do not grow under turbulent conditions such as floods. In fact violent conditions, such as hurricanes, destroy them. The flood described by advocates of a cataclysmic global flood would have been much more violent than any hurricane and would have utterly destroyed these reefs.

Evaporite deposits argue against a global flood that occurred a few thousand years ago. Evaporite deposits contain minerals that are soluble in water, such as halite (sodium chloride or table salt) and sylvite (potassium chloride). According to the generally accepted theory, these deposits are formed slowly by gradual and repeated evaporation of salt water. Such deposits can occur when an arm of a sea is cutoff from the ocean. The water evaporates, and then the depression refills with water from the ocean. This cycle is repeated several times.

If a violent global flood happened, it most likely would have dissolved these most soluble salts.

A turbulent flood should have mixed these soluble minerals with clastic sediments. Unfortunately for the global flood theory, clastic minerals are usually not found in evaporites. Further, pieces of evaporites are not found in clastic sedimentary deposits above or below evaporite deposits. If the global flood theory were valid, evaporite fragments should be found in these sedimentary layers.

Evaporite deposits could not have been formed as a result of the flood waters evaporating and leaving behind a precipitate of salts. Evaporites are found buried under thick clastic sediments not on the surface. Evaporites simply cannot be accounted for by a rapid, one-year process. The great thicknesses involved suggest slow deposition over considerable time.

Dinosaur tracks have been found in lacustrine deposits. If the Flood accounts for the sedimentary rock, how could dinosaurs have left their footprints? Were they walking around in water so torrent that it could move blocks of material weighing thousands of tons?

The sedimentary rock record argues against a universal flood. Although many examples of sedimentary rock formations show evidence of having been formed by moving water, many examples of deposits also show that they could not have formed at all in surging flood waters. These include sedimentary deposits that were evidently formed in lacustrine (lake) and desert environments.

Supporters of a global flood claim that lacustrine deposits occurred during the waning stage of the Flood. Gradual upheaval of the surrounding terrain formed vast sedimentary basins. Shallow turbidity currents carried soft sediment and organic slime into basins to form the laminated sediments. This explanation may explain some lacustrine deposits but not all. Some lacustrine deposits are covered by thick unconsolidated sediments, which would suggest that the Flood was still active in these areas long after it ceased to be active in others.

Eolian deserts argue against a recent global flood. Eolian deserts are the sand dune deserts. They are composed predominately of quartz sand. The sand is well rounded with a frosted surface. Clay and mica are usually absent. A good deal of time is required to erode bedrock to sand and to blow it into dunes. These sandy deserts could not have formed during a global flood.

Many volcanoes argue against a universal flood several thousand years ago. Volcanoes exist that are older than the Flood, no matter which date given in Appendix 1 is used. They show no evidence of being subjected to a highly erosive flood a few thousand years ago.

The catastrophic global flood theory fails to provide a satisfactory answer for fossil coral reefs, evaporite deposits, lacustrine deposits, eolian deserts, and ancient volcanoes. These geological facts are difficult for the advocators of a universal flood to explain away. Other geological facts are impossible to explain away.

A stratum in Yellowstone Park disproves the universal flood theory. The stratum contains successive forests destroyed by lava. Enough time was needed for each forest to mature and then be covered by lava. Time was needed for the lava to weather into soil before the next forest could grow. Much more than a few thousand years are needed for these events to occur.*

Moreover, the orderliness of the sedimentary strata testifies against a universal violent flood. The strata are not homogeneous. They consist of successive layers that differ widely in their contents and character. They are not a jumbled confusion. Land animals are not found in the same strata with fishes. Neither are extinct species found with present species. They lie methodically, each in its own successive sedimentary deposition.† The orderliness of the fossil record does not support a universal flood.

Igneous petrology# also argues against a universal flood. Many examples of magma intruding between layers of fossil-bearing sedimentary rock and crystallizing into igneous rock can be cited. According to the most popular universal flood theory, all fossil-bearing sedimentary rock was formed during the Flood. Thus, these intrusions occurred during or after the Flood. The massive granitic batholiths of California, Idaho, and British Columbia illustrate the fallacy of the universal flood theory. These magma intrusions were so massive that they required hundreds of thousands or even a million years to cool.

---

*Here also is evidence that the fossil record cannot be accounted for by the Flood. At most only one of these forests could have been destroyed during the Flood.

†Occasional exceptions may be found, but orderliness is the rule.

#Igneous petrology is the branch of geology that deals with the development, emplacement, and crystallization of molten rock material, magma, within or on the surface of the Earth.

Such rocks rule out a universal flood of a few thousand years of age unless the Flood was strictly a miraculous event where the physical laws of nature were suspended during the year of the Flood.

Some advocates of a universal flood are honest enough to admit that trying to explain a universal flood using the theories and laws of modern geology and physics is fruitless. In this they agree with those who question a universal flood. They in effect claim that the Flood was a miracle, i.e., God suspended His laws of nature. Biblical suggestions that the Flood was strictly miraculous are extremely weak at best. Only by starting with the premise that the Flood was a miraculous universal event could one arrive at the conclusion that it was.

In summary, the geological and fossil records testify against a universal flood. Where the Bible does refer to geological events related to the Flood, it supports a local flood.

Geography Supports a Local Flood

The Bible strongly suggests that geography was not significantly changed by the Flood. This implication is seen especially in Genesis 2:8-14 with the description of the location of the Garden of Eden. If Noah's flood had been as catastrophic and devastating as the Whitcomb and Morris' flood or Patten's flood, it is highly unlikely that the Tigris and Euphrates, the gold and onyx of Havilah, and even Havilah itself, existed before the Flood. According to their theories and other related universal flood theories, all, or nearly all, fossil-bearing sedimentary rock plus the newer mountains, such as the Himalayan, Rockies, and Andes, were the result of the

Noachian Flood. If their theory is correct, geography before the Flood would differ greatly from geography after the Flood. A geographical description of the location of Eden would be meaningless.

Civilization after the Flood Supports a Local Flood

If the Flood occurred at a late date, such as Usher's date of 2348 B.C., the evidence against a universal flood becomes insurmountable.*

Based on Biblical chronology, Abraham (or Abram as he was called at this time) was born about 2000 B.C. or less than 350 years after the Flood. At the time of his birth, Chaldea was a flourishing country with a large population. Later Abram moved to Canaan. From here he journeyed to Egypt where a great civilization had been established. Egypt also had a dense population at this time.

Ancient Egyptian records do not support a universal flood in the time of Noah. The succession of kings show no interruption from before 3000 B.C. until after 2100 B.C. Further, the Great Pyramid, which was built

---

*Whitcomb and Morris realize the difficulty in presenting a convincing argument for a universal flood in 2348 B.C. that destroyed all mankind and all land animals except for those on the Ark. They expend hundreds of pages attacking geology as a valid science for measuring the age of anything. Yet they turn around and accept archeology as a valid dating science with little or no explanation as to what makes it so superior to geology. After expending hundreds of pages explaining geology using a strict literal reading of Genesis, they reject the Bible's chronology and place the Flood in the sixth millennia B.C.

more than three hundred years before the Flood (with Usher's date), shows no signs of having been covered with water. No indication of the Flood having any impact at all in Egypt is found.

Moreover, the population needed to build the Egyptian civilization with its pyramids and other great structures, to build the civilization of Mesopotamia with its cities and temples, to build the Chinese civilization, and to erect hundreds of massive stone structures in Europe, such as Stonehenge,* and other cities and structures throughout the world, all within a few centuries after the Flood, argues against a universal Flood. According to Biblical chronology and genealogy, no more than a few hundred (if one wants to be overly generous, a few thousand) descendants of Noah were living at the time of the building of the Tower of Babel, which occurred during the third generation from Noah. These descendants were not concentrated in Shinar. Instead, they were scattered across the Middle East, North Africa, and southern Europe. The undertaking of such construction would have required a labor force of millions plus ten to twenty times that number to support

---

*To build Stonehenge took an estimated 1.5 million man-days. The construction of the Tower of Babel took a work force estimated at 600,000 laborers; an estimated one billion man-days were required to plan, build, and decorate the Tower of Babel. If the Flood were universal, the Great Pyramid would have had to have been built after the Flood. It is estimated that 100,000 men working 20 years was needed to build the Great Pyramid. These numbers do not include the labor force needed to feed and otherwise support these massive workforce.

the labor force, not counting people needed for other activities occurring during this period.

Even if the Flood occurred earlier, such as Noorbergen's date of 3398 B.C.,* technology used to build the megalithic monuments, such as Stonehenge and the Great Pyramid, much of which is now unknown, and other great technological advances that occurred within the millennia following the Flood argue against a universal flood. This technology included exploring and mapping the globe accurately and in detail. According to Noorbergen, aviation, missiles and even global nuclear war occurred during this millennium. (Noorbergen dates this nuclear war about 2400 B.C.) Noorbergen believes that most of this technology existed before the Flood. Noah and his family brought the knowledge of this technology through the Flood. Whether he is right or wrong about antediluvian technology is not that important. He notes that the great technological advances that have occurred during the last six hundred years could have occurred in the first six to ten centuries following the Flood. If such great technological advances occurred after the Flood as Noorbergen claims, this fact argues against a universal flood. Even if such great technological advances did not occur after the Flood, those that did occur argue against a universal flood.

A universal flood would have destroyed the global infrastructure. After the Flood, no roads, mines, forests,

---

*Noorbergen believes in a recent universal flood, yet the technology that he describes in his book *Secrets of the Lost Races: New Discoveries of Advanced Technology in Ancient Civilizations* as occurring within a millennia following the Flood are difficult to explain if the Flood were universal.

factories, or farms would have existed. Nothing would have existed except an eroded barren landscape completely alien to the inhabitants of the Ark. Except for Noah and his family, all skilled craftsmen would have died. The only skills remaining would have been those possessed by Noah and his family. They may have known how to make a battery, air plane, or nuclear reactor, but such knowledge does not mean that they had the necessary skills. They lacked the materials and labor (the labor force had been reduced to eight people) to make the last two.*

If the great technological advances that Noorbergen claims happened between 3300 and 2400 B.C. did in fact happen, or even just the technology that conventional historians claim happened, they would have required an infrastructure that could not have existed after a universal flood. One reason that technology has advance so much in the last six hundred years is that it was built upon an existing infrastructure. It did not start from scratch. Agriculture had reached the point that farmers could feed people beyond themselves. Such wealth freed labor for other endeavors. Noah's family would have consumed much of their time and resources providing themselves food, fuel, shelter, clothing, and

---

*No individual today possesses the knowledge and skills to make a simple pencil from scratch. No individual has the knowledge to make all the component parts of a pencil and to make the devices used to make these component parts and component parts of these devices.

other necessities.* Noah's family would have had to wait many years before they could harvest trees for lumber and other wood products. The recent era found vast forests awaiting use. Noah's family had to prospect for coal, copper, iron, and other mineral deposits. They would need to make tools to mine and refine the ore and tools to fabricate the metal into useful products. The recent era had mines and foundries for refining metals. It had skilled craftsmen who could fabricate the refined metals. However, what would have been lacking most following a universal flood would have been labor. While the modern era had a good deal of labor available albeit seldom enough, Noah had only eight workers. To overcome this labor shortage, advocates of a universal flood resort to some unsupportable hypothesis of explosive geometric population growth. A lack of food supply would have prevented such growth. The Flood had destroyed almost every living thing.

If Mars miraculously and suddenly acquired a climate similar to Earth's and if planet Earth sent a spaceship to Mars that was the same size as the Ark with eight people, all of whom were geniuses, and a pair of each animal "kind" found on Earth and all the technology, tools, and books that could be put into it, would Mars have several nuclear powers within a thousand years? Not likely. The first task would be that of survival—food, fuel, shelter, and clothing. The knowledge, skills, tools, and technologies not directly related to these activities in their primitive forms would soon be abandoned and forgotten. Within a few

---

*They could have used the Ark as their dwelling, but the Biblical account suggests that they moved away from the Ark.

generations the regression would be so great that many millennia would have to pass before the people on Mars could build a space ship to reach their moons.

The technology that occurred, whether or not as advanced as Noorbergen claims, during the three millennia preceding the birth of Christ argues against a universal flood.

Furthermore, Genesis 4:20 strongly suggests that the civilization that existed before the Flood existed after it. It suggests that the Flood was not universal and that the descendants of Jabal* lived before and after the Flood. It reads, ". . . he [Jabal] was the father of such as dwell in tents and have cattle." No thought of a flood destroying all descendants of Jabal is expressed in this passage. Likewise, in verse 21, Jubal is described as the "father of all such as handle the harp and pipe." No thought of a catastrophe destroying the descendants of Jubal is expressed. To the contrary, these verses clearly show that Cain's descendants lived after the Flood. In fact the civilization described in Genesis 4:17-24 is presented as though it has continued without interruption since the days of these Cainite patriarchs.

Genesis 10:32 further supports the thought that not all people perished in the Flood. It strongly suggests that not all the people were destroyed by the Flood. It reads, "From them they spread themselves among the nations of the earth after the Flood" (Fenton). If all the people had

---

*By the time of the Flood, the Cainites were probably mostly, if not entirely, Turanians, The descendants of Cain, especially those outside of the Tarim Basin, most likely married Turanians instead of Aryans.

been destroyed, there would have been no nations for them to spread themselves among.

Further, the traditional location of antediluvian civilization is the Middle East—especially in Mesopotamia and Persian Gulf area. If the Flood were global, antediluvian geography should have no resemblance with postdiluvian geography; and many universalists would agree. Therefore, if the Flood were universal, the location of antediluvian civilization becomes one of preference or prejudice.

Civilization testifies against a universal flood. Stonehenge, the Great Pyramid, the Tower of Babel, and other great construction projects support a local flood. Technology also supports a local flood.

Diverseness of Flood Stories Supports a Local Flood

Universalists point to flood stories of other peoples and nations to support their argument for a worldwide flood. The flood story is nearly universal and occurs among many diverse people and in many different locations around the world. Thus, a universal flood must have occurred, and these stories describe that flood; so they claim.

If the Flood were global in scope, it is highly doubtful that it destroyed all of mankind except Noah and the seven for much of the same reason. The almost universality of "flood" stories among many various peoples and localities just as easily supports many survivors of such a flood in various locations.*

The universalists argue that the widespread flood legends can as easily be explained by the principle of diffusion as they can by the principle of tradition. Such a claim is highly questionable. Although most of these stories share a similar broad outline, they differ significantly in details. The difference in these stories are much more noticeable than their similarities. If all these flood stories diffused from some common source, then the hero in these stories should have a similar sounding name in most of them. He does not. The Babylonians called him Ut-Napishtam; the Chaldeans, Xisuthrus; the Sumerians, Ziusudra; the Iranians, Yima; the Greeks and Romans, Decalian or Deucalion; the Hindu, Baisbasbata or Mana; the Chinese, Fa-Ho; the Aztec, Coxcox or Tezpi; the Guarani of Brazil, Tamandaré.†

Moreover, a number of diverse ancient people have stories similar to many of the events experienced by the Israelites under Moses's leadership. These events

---

*Tomas argues that these various flood stories describe the escape of various people from Atlantis when it sank. Hence, the flood story of Genesis and other ancient literature is about the sinking of Atlantis. (Churchward attributes them to the sinking of Mu.)

†Based on the occurrence of flood legends, the catastrophe that destroyed the land of Noah seems to have covered the Earth from about 60° longitude west to about 60° (or possibly 35°) longitude east moving eastward. Flood stories are rare in Africa. Those of the Middle East seem to be derived from the same source as the Biblical account. Those of America and Australia seem to be from independent sources.

included eating manna (although it had different names); an audible voice of a god (or a devil); a god-ruler, spiritual god or devil named Yahu or some similar name; unusual and extended darkness; fire in the sky; etc. Does such commonality mean that all these diverse people descended from the Israelites that Moses lead? Of course not. It means that they had a similar experience.

The nearly universal flood stories suggest that the event that caused the Noachian Flood and destroyed all the people in the land of Noah caused unusual flooding in many parts of the world.

If the Flood destroyed all people except Noah and his family, then all people today are descendants of Noah. If all the races of men are descendants of Noah, then all mankind should have advanced at about the same rate. They have not. Climate cannot explain the great difference in the advancement of the various races. The Indian in America never advanced beyond the Neolithic stage until well after the arrival of the White man. The Australians never advanced beyond the Paleolithic stage until after the arrival of the White man. When the White man immigrated to a new environment, he did not regress to the level of the natives, but he continued to advance and to raise the level of the natives.

Diversity of the flood story testifies against a universal flood. Contrary to the claims of the universalists, the diversity of the flood story supports a local flood, albeit a widespread flood, more than it supports a universal flood.*

---

*Some of these flood stories may be describing floods other than the Noahic Flood.

Jesus' Comments Supports a Local Flood

Supporters of a universal flood like to use Luke 17:26-30 and the corresponding verse in Matthew 24:37-39 to support a universal flood. They claim that Jesus confirms that the Noachian Flood was global as he alludes to it when describing the Second Advent. He states that the Flood destroyed all mankind.

What Jesus is referring to in these verses is that men will be conducting their normal affairs of life without thinking or expecting anything cataclysmic to happen. The Noachian Flood was cataclysmic to those people living when and where it occurred. That Jesus' Second Advent will have a global effect does not prove that the Flood was global because he used it as an analogy of his Second Advent. Only eight people believed God's warning and survived the Flood. Numerous people, many of whom are not believers, perhaps a billion or more, will survive Jesus' Second Advent. If this analogy proves that the Flood was global, it must, to be a legitimate analogy, prove that only believers survive the Second Advent. This interpretation refutes the interpretation generally given to Revelation by the futurist and historicalist that a large number of non-believers will survive the Second Advent.

The universalists seem to ignore Jesus's comments about the days of Lot. Jesus described what happened in the days of Lot as like what happened in the days of Noah. In the days of Lot, all were destroyed in the land of Lot—not all mankind except Lot's family. In the days of Noah, all were destroyed in the land of Noah—not all of mankind except Noah's family. Thus, these passages suggest that the Flood was not universal. Jesus compares the "days of Noah" with the "days of Lot." In both instances the people suffered a catastrophe that "destroyed them all." Yet no one claims that "in the days of Lot" all the people on Earth perished. Only all the people in Sodom and some nearby cities were destroyed. Likewise with the Flood, only the people in the Flood perished, not all the people on Earth.

If the Flood were universal, then a series of miracles is set into motion that make all other miracles, including the great decisive miracle of Christianity, the resurrection of Christ Jesus, pale before them. The physical and biological laws of nature had to be suspended. Some miracle triggered the Flood. As shown above, the laws of geology and physics had to be suspended or rewritten to account for geological formations that occurred within a year. (To account for these geological formations with known processes requires hundreds of thousands of years.) Animals from climates as varied as the Arctic, deserts, and tropical rain forests had to be brought together at one location where to many of them a hostile climate existed. Some of these animals move at a snail's pace, so their migration had to start perhaps before the construction of the Ark. Yet another miracle had to occur when the animals were released. Carnivores had to restrain from eating until the population of their prey was large enough to support them without extinguishing the prey. As evident by the arguments in favor of a local flood, a host of other spectacular miracles had to occur if the Flood were universal. Moreover, God would have had to end His seventh day of rest and again create life forms.

If the Flood were basically a miracle from beginning to end, what need was there for an ark? People and animals surviving a flood in a boat are natural not miraculous. If the Flood were a miracle, would not God have illustrated that it was strictly miraculous by saving Noah, his family, and the animals in some miraculous way, such as rapturing them until the flood waters subsided? That Noah was saved in a natural way strongly supports the belief that the Flood was a natural event.

God uses miracles sparingly. Whenever the natural processes that He created can be used to achieve His purpose, He uses them. Miracles are used only in those situations, such as reconciling man to God, where natural processes cannot be used. On the economy of miracles, Dr. Chalmers said,

> It is remarkable that God is sparing of miracles, and seems to prefer the ordinary processes of nature, if equally effectual for the accomplishment of his purposes. He might have saved Noah and his family by miracles, but He is not prodigal of these; and so He appointed that an ark should be made to bear up the living cargo which was to be kept alive on the surface of the waters; and not only so, but He respects the laws of the animal physiology, as He did those of hydrostatics, in that He put them by pairs into the ark, male and female, to secure their transmission to after ages, and food was stored up to sustain them during their long confinement. In short, He dispenses with miracles when these are not requisite for the fulfillment of His ends; and He never dispenses with the ordinary means when these are fitted, and at the same time sufficient for the occasion.*

---

*Dominick M'Causland, *Adam and the Adamite; or, the Harmony of Scripture and Ethnology* (London, 1858), pp. 217-218.

If the Flood were basically a miraculous event, God would have saved Noah and his family in a miraculous way. Yet He did not. God could have and did accomplish His purpose with the Flood without resorting to a series of miracles.*

If all else fails to persuade, the universalists retort that if the Flood were not global, then the Bible is a collection of fables. A variant of this objection is that if one *really* believes anything in the Bible, he must believe in a global flood: If one does not believe in a global Flood, one does not believe anything in the Bible. This assertion is so absurd that it hardly deserves a comment.

The Flood was local. The Flood story needs to be understood phenomenally. From Noah's perspective on the Ark, all he could see was water. He could see no land. Therefore, water covered all the mountains. He could see no life outside the Ark. Therefore, all life outside the Ark was destroyed. Only as far as the area, observation, and information of Noah extended was the Flood universal.

As discussed below, the purpose of the Flood was to destroy Aryans guilty of miscegenation and their Aryan hybrid offspring. To accomplish its purpose, the Flood did not have to be universal. It needed only to occur

---

*Among the great "miracles" of the Bible is that of timing. If God's command is obeyed when given, the recipient of His command is saved from some natural or manmade disaster. Noah obeyed and was saved. Lot obeyed and was saved, but his wife disobeyed and perished. The exodus of the Israelites is full of the miracle of timing. The Passover and crossing of the Red Sea illustrate that obeying God's command when given results in deliverance. Failure to invade the Promise Land in a timely manner resulted in disaster.

where the polluted Aryans lived. As these Aryans lived in the Tarim Basin and possibly the surrounding area, this is where the Flood was the greatest although its effects were felt over a much larger area.

Where Did the Flood Occur?

When Adam was driven from Eden, he went to the east. The tradition of ancient Chaldea, Egypt, and China identify the first civilization as existing in a region surrounded by high mountains. East of the Pamir is the Tarim Basin of Eastern Turkestan. Eastern Turkestan contains all the conditions necessary for the Flood of Genesis to destroy all the inhabitants within their mountain-enclosed "earth" or country.

Once a large body of water covered this area, which most likely was a gigantic fresh water lake. Apparently at sometime in the past the earth movement that caused the earth to collapse in East Turkestan changed the whole basin into an inland sea.

According to legends in East Turkestan, many cities once existed in this area, but they were buried under a rain of sand as Divine punishment.

The land inhabited by Adamites and Cainites destroyed by the Flood was a valley surrounded by high mountains east of Eden. It was about 1000 miles long. The Flood, earthquakes, and the rising of the region to form a high plateau has enormously changed it. Water covered the highest mountain peaks and overflowed into the surrounding countries. Noah's Ark was stranded on Ararat,* which means "the highest peak."

According to Chinese records, floods occurred east of the Tarim Basin for decades following the Flood. These floods were caused by the drainage of the basin into China. Finally the region dried up, and much of it became a desert.

The universalists claim that the physical phenomena described in Genesis Six through Nine is inconceivable if the Flood had been confined to one section of the Earth. For water to cover even one high mountain in the Near East without inundating Australia and America too would be impossible.

If the Flood occurred in a gigantic valley, such as Tarim Basin, surrounded by high mountains, such as those on the south and west of the Tarim Basin, water could cover the entire land. Even the mountains in that land could be covered. Water could fill the basin until the water flowed over the containing mountains without inundating America or even Australia.

The error made by most advocates of the local flood is that they locate it in the Middle East. For a flood to

---

*The correct location of Ararat is in Eastern Turkestan. Traditionalists locate it in Turkey. When Noah and his family migrated to Shinar they brought with them the story of the Flood. Noah came from the north and east. As the people of Shinar retold the story of the Flood, they associated the mountain on which the Ark landed with the highest mountain to the north. Being familiar with the mountains of Turkey, they named the highest mountain there Ararat. They were ignorant of the Himalayas and adjacent mountains to the north of the Himalayas.

occur in that region high enough to cover the highest mountains of that region without it being nearly universal would be difficult.

2 Peter 3:5, 6 reads, "For this they wilfully forget, that there were heavens from of old, and an earth compacted out of water and amidst [or through] water, by the word of God; by which means the world that then was, being overflowed with water, perished." These verses are used to support a universal flood. Some universalists interpret "the world that then was, being overflowed with water, perished" as identifying the location of the antediluvian civilization as the Pacific Basin. If the Pacific Basin is the location of antediluvian civilization, does this mean that the continent of Mu was real? Why not Atlantis in the Atlantic Ocean. The geology of the Atlantic Ocean supports a sunken continent theory better than the geology of the Pacific Ocean. Also, these verses do not proclaim a universal flood. They do affirm God's creative powers and castigate those who deny His being and who deny His coming judgment. The Adamic world of Noah is what perished with the Flood—not the entire planet.

All the evidence points to the Tarim Basin as the location of the Flood. No other place on Earth fits the Scriptural description of the land of Noah as well as the Tarim Basin.

The Rainbow

Many universalists argue that the rainbow was a phenomenon that did not occur on the planet until after the Flood. The great watery canopy prevented the Sun's rays from reaching the Earth's surface. The Sun illuminated the canopy (thus the "greater light" by day (Gen. 1:16)). When this canopy vanished with the Flood, the Sun's rays could reach the Earth's surface. Sunlight refracting through water drops could now be seen as a rainbow.

Genesis 9:13 reads, "I do set my bow in the cloud, and it shall be for a token of a covenant between me and the earth." This verse does not claim that God created the rainbow following the Flood. *Bārā* is the Hebrew word for "create." It claims that God set (*nâthan*) the rainbow. Here "set" is used in the sense of "make," "give," or "appoint." So, God gave the rainbow as a sign or symbol of His covenant and mercy.

God makes the rainbow as a sign of His covenant. Does this mean that the first appearance of the rainbow on the planet Earth occurred after the Flood? No. Using the rainbow as a sign of His covenant, God attached a religious significance to it. To argue otherwise is to claim that no man was circumcised until Abraham and that no one was baptized until Jesus. Men were circumcised before Abraham. People were baptized before Jesus. Like the rainbow, they achieved significance when they became symbolic of God's covenant.

Rainbows existed before the Flood. After the Flood, they served a new function. They became a symbol to man that God would never again bring such a Flood. The rainbow is symbolic of God's covenant with Noah and his descendants. It symbolizes the binding of man to God in a covenant relationship. Man is obliged to obey God's moral law. For His part, God promises to sustain the Earth and make provision for Noah and his descendants and the other inhabitants of Earth. The rainbow is a token of God's provincial care.

Why Did God Send the Flood

Why did God send the Flood? The short answer is sin. One sin is named: miscegenation (Genesis 6:2). The sons of God cohabited with the daughters of man. This sin led to other sins until "Jehovah saw that the wickedness of man was great in the earth, and that every imagination of the thoughts of his heart was only evil continually" (Genesis 6:9). The Flood served as a cataclysmic judgment upon the wicked and as salvation for Noah and his family.

In the sixth chapter the miscegenation occurs between the "sons of God" and the "daughters of man." The question arises about who were the sons of God and the daughters of man. Some have believed that the sons of God were the nobility or patricians while the daughters of man were the peasants or plebeians. Others understand that the sons of God refer to angels.* Still others claim that the sons of God were the Sethites and the daughters of man were the Cainites. Some believe that the sons of God refer to truly pious men, worshipers of the true God, who are usually thought of as being Sethites, while the daughters of man referred to the worldly people, who are usually thought of as being Cainites. Another possibility is that Genesis 6:2 means the Adamites were intermarrying with pre-Adamic man

---

*Angels are called the sons of God in Job 1:6 and 38:7. In these passages the sons of Gods are unfallen angels. If such an unholy thought or desire as having sexual relations with the daughters of Adam had entered the minds of these unfallen angels, God would have sent them to Tartarus (2 Peter 2:4) where He sent the angels who rebelled with Satan. Further, how could spiritual beings like angels perish in a flood?

or the hybrid Cainites in large numbers. This last explanation is most likely the correct one. The great sin that led to the Flood was the Adamites integrating with and marrying pre-Adamic man and possibly hybrid Cainites.*

Were the "sons of God" the Adamites, or were the "daughters of man" the Adamites? If the sons of God were Adamites, then this phrase would refer to men created in the image of God. It could not mean righteous or pious men because such men would not commit the sin of miscegenation en masse. More likely the daughters of man refer to the Adamites. Perhaps a more literal translation of Genesis 6:2 is "that the sons of God saw the daughters of the Adamites that they were fair. . . ." This translation shows that the daughters of man were daughters of Adamites, i.e., they were Aryans. Another clue that the daughters of man were Aryans is that they were fair. Only Aryans are fair. If the daughters of men refer to Aryans, then the sons of God refer to pre-Adamic man, who were most likely Turanians, although they also could have been Melanochroi, for Nephilim, a Melanochroic people, were in the land at this time (Genesis 6:4). If the sons of God refer to pre-Adamic man, then a more accurate rendering of the phrase is "sons of the gods." Hence, it means idolaters, worshipers of false

---

*As the purpose of the Flood was to destroy all the Adamite hybrids, the Aryans who had earlier emigrated from the Tarim Basin to regions not impacted by the Flood must not have mixed with the other species of men. Noah and his family were among the few who had maintained their racial integrity. Because the Aryan emigrants had maintained their racial integrity, the Flood did not have to be universal.

gods. Pre-Adamic men would have been worshipers of false gods, for they were not created in the image of God. If this translation is correct, this phrase could still refer to pre-Adamic man. This phrase is used to express the thought of greatness. It could, therefore, refer to men of great stature, strength, or renown. Whether the "sons of God" or the "daughters of man" refer to the Aryans, the result is the same. Miscegenation was a great sin that the Flood was sent to purge.

Purpose of the Ark

The universalists ask why God would direct Noah to spend 120 years to build a huge boat if the Flood only covered a limited area? Could not he and his family have reached safety by simply leaving the area to be flooded? One explanation is that God wanted to give the people plenty of time to repent. On judgment day they cannot argue that they were not warned. (If the Flood were global, there would have been many people beyond Noah's warning.) God ordered a large boat built to show that He was willing and able to save all who believed and repented. On the symbolic nature of the Flood, the Bishop of Ely wrote,

> If it be inquired why it pleased God to save man and beast in a large vessel, instead of leaving them a refuge on high hills, or in some other sanctuary, we, perhaps, inquire in vain. Yet surely we can see that the great moral lesson and the great spiritual truths exhibited in the deluge and the ark were well worth a signal departure from the common course of nature and Providence. The judgment was far more marked, the deliverance far more manifestly Divine, than they would have been if hills or trees or caves had been the shelter provided for those to be saved.

> The great prophetic forepicturing of salvation from a flood of sin by Christ and in the church of Christ would have lost all its beauty and symmetry, if merely earthly refuges had been sufficient for deliverance. As it is, the history of Noah, next after the history of Christ, is that which most forcibly arrests our thoughts, impresses our consciences, and yet revives our hopes. It was a judgment signally executed at the time. It is a lesson deeply instructive for all time.*

Like so many other stories in the Old Testament, the story of the Flood symbolizes God's saving grace through Christ.

---

*[William H. Campbell], *Anthropology for the People: A Refutation of the Theory of the Adamic Origin of All Races* (Richmond, 1891), pp. 199-200.

6
FOLLOWING THE FLOOD

Many historians have identified the high grasslands of Central Asia north of the great Asian mountain zone as the cradle of the Aryan people. Out of this region came the Adamic race. The Adamic race was the builder of ancient civilizations. They brought writing and the arts and astronomy, mathematics, and other sciences. They brought the natives advancements that they were incapable of producing on their own. Part of the arts and sciences of civilization they brought non-Adamic man before the Flood. Part they brought after the Flood.

Like many of their ancestors before the Flood, Noah and his family migrated out of Eastern Turkestan to Central Asia in the region of the Oxus River. Here and along the way they most likely encountered other Adamites that had migrated to this region long before the Flood. They led some of these Aryans southward and westward toward Mesopotamia and Egypt.

They reenforced the civilization in Sumer, and brought enlightened and advanced civilizations to Egypt and other areas of the Middle East. The civilization that they brought included an alphabet and writing, which is the most important tool of an advanced civilization. These civilizations also possessed knowledge of mathematics, astronomy, metallurgy, and other sciences. They had a system for measuring time, distance, and weight. Their architecture, arts, and agriculture had advanced well beyond that of the Neolithic people that they found.

The Descendants of Noah

The tenth chapter of Genesis should be viewed as an ethnographical record instead of an ethnological record. It describes various geographical areas where the descendants of Noah, i.e., the tribes of one racial stock, settled. In no way does it describe in any manner the creation of races from the division of a single parent stock. The areas mentioned in the tenth chapter of Genesis do not include any areas inhabited by Negroes or Turanians at that time. It describes geographical areas, not racial connections. Except for Nimrod and possibly Peleg, the names following Noah's three sons are geographical-ethnological personifications. They are names of peoples, tribes, and nationalities instead of individuals.

As the descendants of Noah migrated into the Middle East, they divided into three parts. The Japhethites migrated to northern Iran, southern Russia, Asia Minor, and Greece, and along the northern Mediterranean to Spain. The Shemites migrated into Syria, Mesopotamia, Arabia and southwest Persia. The Hamites migrated to Palestine, Arabia and north Africa.

Some of these descendants may have acquired the name of the region in which they settled or the people among whom they settled. Some of the people among whom they settled or regions in which they settled may have acquired the name of Noah's descendants.

The Japhethites

The Indo-Europeans are descended from Japheth. The immediate descendants of Japheth listed in chapter ten of Genesis are Gomer, Magog, Madai, Javan, Tubal, Meshech, and Tiras.

Gomer* settled in Crimea and the region north of the Black Sea. Gomer is related to Cimmerians and Celts.

The Bible mentions three tribes that descended from Gomer: Ashkenaz, Riphath, and Togarmah. Ashkenaz lived in Mysia and Phrygia in Asian Minor. They later migrated to western Armenia (Jeremiah 51:27). Some mistakenly identify the Ashkenazic Jews of Central Europe as descendants of Ashkenaz; they are descended from the Khazars. Ashkenaz is associated with the Phrygians, Germans, Saxons, and possibly the Basque. Riphath may have lived in the region of modern-day Hungary and Rumania and perhaps Great Britain and France. Riphath is associated with the Wends, Slavic Prussians, and possibly other Slavic people, and the Lithuanians. Togarmah lived in Armenia (Ezekiel 27:14; 38:6) and is identified with the Armenians, Georgians, Iranians, Lesgians, Mingrelians, and Caucasians.

Magog settled in the region north of the Black Sea to the north of the Caspian Sea. Magog is related to the

---

*For the most part, the Biblical names of Noah's descendants should be thought of as names of tribes or a people rather than a name of an individual although the original chief or founder of the tribe may have had this name.

Scythians and Khazars† and possibly to the Getae, Alans, and Ossetes.

Madai settled in northern Persia (Iran) south of the Caspian Sea. Madai is related to the Medes and Iranians.

Javan settled in southern Greece and the islands of the Aegean Sea. Javan is related to the Ionians.

The Bible mentions five tribes or lands associated with Javan: Elishah, Tarshish, Kittim (or Chittim), Dodanim (or Rodanim), and Isles of the Gentiles. Elishah was the Aeolians, who inhabited Crete, Cyprus, the isles of the Aegean Sea, and the coastline of Asia Minor. The Carthaginians may have also been kin to Elishah. Some scholars identify Tarshish with Tarsus in Cilicia, but most identify it with the coast of southern Spain. A few believe the Etruscans of Italy descended from Tarshish. Most scholars identify Kittim with Cyprus although some identify it with Italy or Macedonia. Dodanim† were the Dardanians from whom the Trojans descended. The Isles of the Gentiles referred to the Japhetic colonies on the coast of the Mediterranean, Black, and Caspian Seas.

Tubal settled along the southern shores of the Black Sea and present-day Georgia. Tubal is related to the Tibareni, Iberians (Asian Iberians, not the Spanish), and Georgians.

---

*Most of the modern-day Jews are descended from the Khazars and not from the Israelites.

†Dodanim is named in Genesis 10:4 whereas Rodanim is named in the parallel verse in 1 Chronicles 1:7. Rodanim probably referred to the Isle of Rhodes. Some scholars have identified Rodanim with the Rhone river, which has lead some to conclude that France is the country of Rodanim.

Meshech settled between the Black and Caspian Seas above the Moschian Mountains. Meshech is related to the Moschi.

Tiras settled southwest of the Black Sea. Tiras is related to the Thracians. Some scholars believe that the Etruscans came from Tiras. Also the Turusha, a seafaring people, and the Tyrseni, a people dwelling on the shores of the Aegean Sea, may have descended from Tiras.

The Hamites

The Hamites descended from Ham.* The immediate descendants of Ham listed in chapter ten are: Cush, Mizraim, Phut, and Canaan.

Cush settled in Arabia.† Cush settled among the Melanochroic Arabic tribes of southern Arabia. The Bible identifies five tribes with Cush: Seba, Havilah, Sabtah, Raamah, and Satechah. These people lived in southern Arabia. Nimrod is also mentioned as a descendant of Cush.

---

*Ham was defied as the Egyptian god Khen.

†Most people erroneously identify Cush with the region south of Egypt. The confusion has been caused by the Septuagint and Vulgate translators translating "Cush" as "Ethiopia." The English translators of the Authorized Version followed this traditional translation of the Roman Catholic Church, and translated "Cush," "Cushite," and "Cushites" as "Ethiopia," "Ethiopian," and "Ethiopians" 34 times. For Scriptural proof that the location of Cush is Arabia instead of Nubia or Ethiopia, see *Integration Is Genocide* by Thomas Allen.

Mizraim* settled in Egypt. The Bible mentions six tribes kin to Mizraim: Ludim, Anamim, Lehabim, Naphtuhim, Pathrusim, Casluhim and Caphtorim.

The location of Ludim is uncertain. Some have identified it with Nubia, which is doubtful. Others have identified it with the Lydians of Asia Minor, which is also doubtful. The most probable location of Ludim is along the Barbary coast into the Sahara—especially in Morocco. Many of the Berbers of northern Morocco are related to Ludim.

Anamim lived in Algeria. Many of the Berbers of Algeria related to Anamim.

Lehabim are also called Lubim and Libyans in the Bible. They lived west of Egypt in present-day Libya along the shores of the Mediterranean.

Naphtuhim lived around Memphis and along the western frontier of Egypt. The Berbers of eastern Libya and western Egypt descended from Naphtuhim.

Pathrusim, also called Pathros by the prophets, lived in Upper Egypt according to some scholars or in Pharusia in Barbary according to others.

Casluhim may have lived in the vicinity of Goshen or, more likely, the Barbary. The Shillouhs are related to Casluhim. Another people often, but probably incorrectly, associated with Casluhim are the Philistim, who lived in southwest Palestine.

Caphtorim are believed to have lived on Crete. The Philistim are more correctly associated with the Caphtorim.

---

*Some scholars identify Mizraim with Menes. Some believe that Menes was a contemporary of Nimrod.

Phut settled in Libya along the Mediterranean and perhaps along the coast of the Maghreb. Phut is related to many of the Berber tribes of North Africa.

Canaan settled in Palestine and Lower Syria. Canaan is related to the Phoenicians and Carthaginians. The Bible identifies, along with the Canaanite people, six tribes in Palestine descending from or related to Canaan: Perizzites, Jebusites, Amorites, Hivites, Girgashites, and Hethites (or Hittites). Other people that the Bible associates with Canaan were the Sidonians, Arkites, Sinites, Arvadites, Zemarites, and Hamathites. These people lived north of Palestine; they are of cities founded by Canaanites or tribes related to the Canaanites.

Curse of Canaan

According to Genesis 9:20-27, Noah became drunk and fell asleep naked. Ham saw his father asleep naked and told his brothers, Shem and Japheth. Shem and Japheth covered their father by walking backwards with the cover so that they would not see his nakedness. Noah awoke and became angry at what Ham had done and pronounced a curse on Ham's son Canaan.

Why did Noah curse Canaan instead of Ham? Various explanations have been offered to explain Noah's curse of Canaan. One explanation is that Ham either slept with Noah's wife or attempted to do so. This explanation has few supporters, and the Scriptures do not support it. Another explanation is that Ham had intercourse with a non-Adamic woman on the Ark. So Noah vented his anger on Canaan. This explanation is inconsistent with the character of the men of the Old Testament. They were direct in their dealings. If Ham had vexed Noah, Noah would have cursed Ham instead of Canaan. A third explanation is that Canaan committed or attempted to commit a homosexual act on Noah while he slept. Some commentators believe that the curse of Canaan is symbolic: It is a curse pronounced on Canaan because the Canaanites corrupted the pure Israelite worship by degrading and drunken orgies of Canaanite Baal-worship. Another explanation is that Canaan first saw Noah naked, and Ham checked Canaan's story and saw Noah naked. All these explanations seem to fall short of the mark.

The answer to the question of why Noah cursed Canaan lies in whom Canaan was that caused Noah's outrage. Looking on his grandfather's naked body is unlikely to have caused such a reaction. Greater vileness than this action was necessary to precipitate Noah's curse. The most reasonable answer to this question is that Canaan was a mongrel. He was the son of Ham by a non-Adamic woman. (She would have been a wife or concubine acquired after the Flood.) Canaan may have also married a non-Adamic woman. His descendants do seem to have intermarried with the non-Adamic inhabitants of Palestine.

The Shemites

The Shemites are descended from Shem. The immediate descendants of Shem listed in chapter ten of Genesis are Elam, Asshur, Arphaxad, Lud, and Aram.

Elam settled in the region east of the Tigris and north of the Persian Gulf.

Asshur settled along the Tigris in the region of Nineveh. Asshur is associated with the Assyrians.

Arphaxad (or Arpachshad) settled in Shinar, primarily in the region of Ur. Related to Arphaxad are the Chaldeans. The Bible identifies Salah with Arphaxad.

The location of Salah is disputed; some place Salah in Elam (Susiana).

From Salah came Eber, who settled in Upper Mesopotamia. From Eber came the Hebrews. The Bible identifies two people as descending from Eber: Peleg* and Joktan. From Joktan came 13 Arabic tribes.†

Lud settled in southwest Asia Minor. Lud is related to the Lydians.

Aram settled in the region bounded by Canaan and Phoenicia on the east, the Euphrates on the north, and the great desert on the west and south. Aram is related to the Syrians (also called Aramaeans). The Bible identifies four tribes or peoples with Aram: Uz, Hul, Gether, and Mash.#

Nimrod

The most famous descendant of Cush is Nimrod. He is credited with founding Babylon and Nineveh. He

---

*Peleg means "split." His name could be symbolic of a splitting or division. The splitting or division is uncertain. However, it could refer to some natural disaster like an earthquake. It could refer to a partition of territory between the Pelegians and Joktanites. Peleg may have been a contemporary of Nimrod. If so, his name could symbolize the fall of Nimrod's empire, which was caused by the confusion of languages resulting from the Tower of Babel. Unger dates Peleg as living while the Tower of Babel was being built.

†See Genesis 10:26-29 for the names of these tribes.

#In 1 Chronicles 1:17, these four are listed as sons of Shem. In Genesis 10:23 they are listed as sons of Aram.

founded the Babylonian Empire. He originated the military state and was one of a long line of warrior-kings of Babylonia and Assyria. The Tower of Babel is his most famous architectural work. Some believe that he founded Freemasonry. Renowned for his evilness, he led his people in rebellion against God, and God destroyed his empire.* His was an empire of depravity, lust, violence, and genocide. A practitioner of the occult, he attempted to elevate man to the level of God. All the horrors of despotism and tyranny that twentieth century man has come to know first hand, Nimrod practiced. (Such is life when man supplants Jehovah with himself as god.) Nimrod was the epitome of evil. He was truly a disciple of Satan.

Some believe that Nimrod was of mixed race. According to Mullins, his consort was Naamah. She was a Nephilim and was known for her beauty, talent, energy, lustfulness, and cruelty. She taught him the practice of ritual murder and cannibalism. Naamah taught him that sacrificing and eating fair-skinned people would enhance his parlous and power and give his children the superior qualities of the White race.

Nimrod is often identified as Marduk, Bel, and Merodach. He has also been associated with the gods Ninurta and Orion. He has been identified as Gilgamesh, a legendary king of Babylonia.

---

*Some scholars believe that Elam, son of Shem and father of the Elamites, overthrew Nimrod's empire. Others believe that Arphaxad overthrew him.

Post-Flood Migration of Aryans

About 3200 B.C. Aryans came out of Turkestan and crossed Iran to the Lower Mesopotamia. Their arrival coincided with the advent of the Bronze Age and writing. They were the people who were identified in the Bible as the descendants of Shem and Ham.* These people settled in Elam and Arabia along the Persian Gulf. Here they remained for some centuries and acquired the Hamitic and Semitic languages of the Melanochroi living there.† Many of these people integrated and intermarried with the more numerous Melanochroi and lost their racial integrity and identity. Those who did not amalgamate and assimilate with the Melanochroi amalgamated and assimilated more or less with the Aryans of the region.

---

*The descendants of Japheth traveled the route across northern Iran that the Hittites would later follow. They settled among related people in the northern part of the Middle East.

†Alternatively, these Aryans spoke Semetic and Hamitic languages, or the ancestor of these languages, before arriving in the Middle East. If so, they gave their languages to the native Melanochroi among whom they settled. Both Aryans and Melanochroi spoke Semetic languages. Semetic and Hamitic languages are related. With the exception of the Aryans of the Maghreb, Hamitic languages are spoke exclusively by Melanochroi. Therefore, both Semetic and Hamitic languages were probably languages of the Melanochroi. Aryans acquired Semetic languages by living close to or under the authority (political, economic, or both) of more numerous Semetic speaking Melanochroi. Alternatively, Indo-European languages and Semetic and Hamitic languages may have had a common ancestor, and the invading Aryans superimposed their language on the indigenous population.

One of the tribes of these Aryans was the Mizraim. About 3200 B.C. the Mizraim, a predominately Mediterranean people, moved into Lower Egypt. They probably infiltrated in small bands rather than coming as a conquering herd. Not long after their arrival in Lower Egypt, some of them moved into Upper Egypt. One of their kings in Upper Egypt, Menes, united Lower and Upper Egypt under his rulership (c. 3100 B.C.) Most of the Mizraim, however, remained in Lower Egypt.

About 2850 B.C. the Pre-Sumerian Elamites of Babylonia had become so weak that they enticed the Chaldeans, a Melanochroic Eastern-Hamite people, to attack. The Chaldeans came out of Arabia, conquered Sumer and Agade, and, thereby, made themselves the dominant power in Babylonia. Toward Syria the Sumerians fled. The Akkadians later overthrew the Chaldeans and conquered Babylonia (c. 2450 B.C.).

A tribe of Mediterranean people who had settled in Arabia came up the shore of the Persian Gulf and invaded Upper Mesopotamia around 2800 B.C. These people were known as the Akkadians.* They conquered the northwestern part of Babylonia and established a settlement near where modern Bagdad is located. Mesopotamia was now divided into a northern kingdom, Akkad, and southern kingdom, Sumer.

About 2300 B.C. the Turanians of Central Asia began moving east, north, and west. To the north they encountered the Ugrian Turanians, who moved across the Irtysh River and southward toward Lake Balkhash. Their

---

*Akkadians were a Mediterranean Aryan people who spoke a Semetic language.

southerly movement caused the Nordic Aryans living between Lake Balkhash and Eastern Turkestan to move. This Nordic movement caused the Aryan Hittites* living in Western Turkestan to migrate westward.

This movement of Turanians and Hittites precipitated another great migration of Celts out of the Pamirs. Turanians and Hittites pushed most of the Alpine Aryans out of the mountain valleys of Western Turkestan (c. 2300 B.C.). These Alpines were the Celto-Slavs. They fled west with the Hittites pursuing. When the Celto-Slavs passed around the southern shores of the Caspian Sea, they crossed the Caucasus Mountains and moved north while the Hittites continued west to Anatolia.

As the Celto-Slavs moved northward, they divided. One group, who became known as the Muscovites (Slavs), continued north while the other group moved westward along the northern shores of the Black Sea and up the Danube River. This latter group became known as the Neo-Celts or the "Battle-Ax Folks." The Celto-Slavs spread across eastern and central Europe and amalgamated with the Paleo-Celts and often with other Aryan people of Europe. They became the progenitors of the Alpines and Slavs of eastern and central Europe.

About 2300 B.C. the Aryan Hittites invaded Anatolia and established an empire there. When they came across northern Iran, the Chaldeans of Babylonia and the Assyrians of Upper Mesopotamia prevented them from entering the Fertile Crescent. So they swerved westward, crossed over the highlands, and settled in north central

---

*Hittites were predominantly of the Armenian type, who were related to the Alpine Aryans.

Anatolia where they subjected the Hatti of central Anatolia to their rule. Their invasion of Anatolia drove out most, if not all, of the Aryan Kassites, Leleges, Caucones, and Pelasgians living there. The first two people were descendants of the Pre-Sumerians, and the last two were descendants of the Mediterraneans who had earlier settled in Anatolia. The Hittites who came to Anatolia consisted primarily of three tribes: the Hittites, Palaicians, and Luwians. The Hittites settled in Cappadocia; the Palaicians, in Bithynia; and the Luwians, in Lycaonia.

The Hittite invasion drove the Mediterranean Caucones and Pelasgians out of central Anatolia. While the Caucones fled to the southern shores of the Black Sea, the Pelasgians fled across the Kizilirmak (Halys River). Some Pelasgians fled as far as the coast of the Aegean Sea while others moved up the Balkans as far as southern Russia.

As a result of the Hittite conquest of central Anatolia, the Leleges were driven into and beyond the Taurus Mountains and became concentrated along the coast. They were a commercial people. Before 3000 B.C. they had become a principal power of the Aegean and east Mediterranean. Their colonies and settlements extended from the Hellespont to the Syrian and Palestinian coast. Their commercial routes extended to the British Isles and Scandinavia. The Leleges had colonies and outposts scattered across much of coastal Europe with mines in Iberia, France, and Cornwall. Ports around the Gulf of Alexandretta were their centers of operation. The concentration of their population along the coast as a result of the Hittite invasion renewed their maritime adventures. As a result the Leleges again extended their commercial activity and settlements across the Aegean Sea and to the western Mediterranean.

About 2500 B.C., or perhaps earlier, another power arose in the eastern Mediterranean to rival the Leleges. This power was the Cretans, the Mediterraneans who had fled Egypt centuries earlier. While the Leleges dominated the trade along the west coast of Asia and the north coast of Africa, the Cretans dominated the trade along the northern shores of the Mediterranean as far west as Italy.

As the Hittites came across northwest Iran, they set in motion another Pre-Sumerian people, the Hurrians. Between 2200 and 1600 B.C., the Hurrians overran northern Mesopotamia and Syria. They carried away many of the tribes whom they conquered. A group of Hurrians, the Hyksos conquered Egypt about 1775 B.C. Many Hurrians eventually perished through intermarriage with the Melanochroic Canaanites.

About 2050 B.C. the Amorites came out of western Palestine and conquered all Babylonia. After the Amorites conquered Babylonia, they banished the Sumerians of Babylonia to Aram and Assyria. Amorites ruled Babylonia until about 1926 B.C. when the Assyrians aided by the Hittites and banished Sumerians successfully seceded from Babylonia. The Assyrians then aided the Sumerians in regaining control of Babylonia. However, the Sumerian rule of Babylonia was short-lived, for about 1780 B.C. the Kassites conquered it.

A tribe of people known as the Hebrews settled in the Babylonian plain about 2050 B.C. near Ur. They were a tribe related the Kassites, i.e., they were a blend of Kassites with the Semitic tribe Eber. They left Ur about 2000 B.C. and settled among the Aryan Aramaeans in Padan-Aram, which was in the upper part of the Fertile

Crescent, in present-day Syria. Like the Kassites, the Aramaeans were also related to the Hebrews. Being closely related, intermarriages between the Hebrews and Aramaeans were frequent, so much so that the Hebrews are often considered a branch of the Aramaeans.

Abraham

Around 2000 B.C., a tribe of Hebrews left the region of Ur.* Ur was the capital of Sumer and a thriving commercial city, with exceptionally high cultural standards. Under the leadership of their chief, Terah (Genesis 11:31) they migrated northward. Political convulsion in southern Mesopotamia probably precipitated Terah's migration.† Possibly an Elamite invasion caused Terah and his band to leave Ur. Terah lead his people to Haran,# which is in the northern part of the fertile crescent. Terah moved from Ur after his son

---

*Ur was most likely the ancient city of Uru, which is located at the modern city of Mugheir. Mugheir is near the Euphrates, 125 miles northwest of the Persian Gulf.

†Akkad was called Uri in Akkadian inscription. Haran was a town in this province. If Ur in Genesis 10:31 refers to the providence of Uri instead of the city of Ur, no need remains to explain why Terah would journey 600 miles from Ur in southern Babylonia to Haran.

#Both Haran and Ur were centers of worship of Sin (or Nanna), the Semite moon-god. Terah apparently worshiped Sin.

Haran died. Along with his sons Nahor and Abram* and his grandson Lot, son of Haran, Terah migrated to Haran.

At Haran the band divided. Part of the band migrated southwestward and founded Damascus. A small portion of this group under the leadership of Abram (Abraham) migrated to Palestine. After Terah died, God told Abram to go to the land of the Canaanites. Abram then took his wife Sarai (Sarah), his nephew Lot, and their servants to Palestine.

---

*Scripture describes Abram as a "son" of Terah. The word "son" is often used in the sense of descendant. Thus, Abram may have been more distantly removed from Terah than a son.

7
ASTRAL CATASTROPHISM

What is set out in this chapter is an overview of the Astral Catastrophe Theory as described by Patten. The dates are Patten's.

During one era of Earth's history, many astronomical cataclysms occurred. This era ended in 701 B.C. Between the Flood and the last catastrophe in 701 B.C., the cause of these catastrophes was Mars or Venus.* During this era Mars had an orbit that crossed the Earth's orbit. Its gravitational pull reeked havoc on Earth. In all there were eight major encounters and several minor ones during this time. According to Patten, the major ones were:

1. Tower of Babel	1930 B.C.
2. Sodom-Gomorrah	1877
3. Exodus	1447
4. Long Day of Joshua	1404
5. Greater Davidic	972
6. Joel-Amos	756
7. Isaiahic	701

---

*Patten believes that all these catastrophes were caused by Mars. Velikovsky believes that while some were caused by Mars, many were caused by Venus.

The minor catastrophes included:

1.	Peleg	2146 B.C.
2.	Job	1663
3.	Deborah Debacle	1188
4.	Samuelic	1080
5.	Lesser Davidic	1025
6.	Elijahic	864

These catastrophes have been determined from the charting of the orbits of Mars by the ancients and comparing the movements of Mars with the Hebrew historical records, the Bible, and other sources, and with the histories, literature, and myths of the ancients. Although Patten credits Mars with causing the postdiluvian catastrophes, he credits Mercury with causing the Noahic Flood.

Among the things resulting from these catastrophes were changes in the Earth's orbit, i.e., changing the number of days for the Earth to revolve around the Sun, reversal of the geomagnetic field, changes in the precession or wobble of the spin axis, relocation of the geographical poles, changes in the tilt, and changes in spin rate. Some caused changes in the Moon's orbit.

Tower of Babel Catastrophe

The Tower of Babel catastrophe occurred about October 25, 1930 B.C. The Tower was probably destroyed by shock waves from exploding bolides. This catastrophe caused a mass migration of people out of Shinar. Genesis 11:6-8 describes the Tower of Babel catastrophe. These verses suggest that the Tower was destroyed from above by cosmic forces from heaven. No indication is given that an invading army or a riotous crowd sacked and burned the Tower.

Peleg Catastrophe

The Peleg catastrophe occurred about 2146 B.C. Peleg was born c. 2168 B.C. and died c. 1929 B.C. According to Genesis 10:25, the Earth was divided during his day. This division was caused by a new equatorial zone of oblateness. The Flood catastrophe caused a shift in the poles of perhaps three thousand to five thousand miles. The shift in the poles resulted in a new equator. From the Earth's mean diameter, the equatorial zone bulges out about 26 miles. Because of the shift in the poles, the bulge of the old equatorial zone had to migrate to the new equatorial zone. That is, the old zone shrank and the new zone grew. Numerous earthquakes were the result.

The Flood Catastrophe

The Flood catastrophe occurred circa 2400 to 2500 B.C. It was caused by Mercury and its icy satellite. A pair of catastrophes caused the Flood. These events occurred over a 150-day period. The first event occurred about November 7 when Mercury passed between 25,000 and 30,000 miles of Earth. Its icy satellite fragmented and drenched the Earth with an average of 200 to 250 inches of rain per square inch. About half the ice particles hit the Earth as sudden rain. The remainder of the ice particles formed rings around the Earth like the rings around Saturn. These icy particles proceeded to descend over the geomagnetic polar regions in a deep sub-zero icy mist over the next 35 to 40 days. (This was the 40 days and nights of rain.) This interaction between Mercury and Earth caused the geographical poles to shift between twenty-five hundred and three thousand miles. It also caused the uplifting of the entire Circum-Pacific cycle of mountains.

The second event occurred about March 20 or 30 when Mercury passed even closer to the Earth. This pass caused the uplifting of the Alpine-Himalayan cycle of mountains. It also shifted the geographical poles another three thousand to thirty-five hundred miles, reset the vernal equinox, and again reversed the geomagnetic field.

Enosh Catastrophe

There appears to have been a catastrophe during the generation of Enosh. (Enosh's generation was the first idol worshipers.) This catastrophe was in the form of tidal waves.

Pre-Adamic Catastrophe

A catastrophic era appears to have occurred before the creation of Adam. These catastrophes formed the older mountains, e.g., the Herzian-Calendionian cycle, and created strata not attributable to the Flood (Proverbs chapter 8 and Job chapter 38).

Canopy Theory

According to the canopy theory, the Earth was, before the Flood, surrounded by a canopy of water, i.e., a thick layer of water vapor or ice above the troposphere. This canopy of water vapor created a greenhouse effect. Before the Flood a canopy of water vapor surrounded the Earth. This canopy allowed only slight variations in temperature with latitude and altitude. Atmospheric turbulence was almost nonexistent. Large movements of air masses were absent. Rain did not occur. Vegetation was watered by a mist, something similar to fog.

Many supporters of the global flood theory and many supporters of the astral catastrophe theory support the canopy theory. The non-catastrophic universalists claim that something caused the water in this canopy to precipitate, while something else caused the surface water to rise and groundwater to erupt from the Earth thus covering the whole Earth with water. Later the Earth's surface where the oceans are now located sank to create a reservoir into which water drained, thereby giving dry land. The catastrophic universalists claim that a planet, asteroid, or similar heavenly body passed near the Earth and caused the water in the canopy to precipitate. Perhaps more water was added from an exploding satellite while the gravitational pull of the passing body caused tidal waves miles high to wash over the land. A basic difference between the two schools is the mechanism used to destroy the canopy.

To prove that a watery canopy surrounded the planet before the Flood, its supporters quote 2 Peter 3:5,6, which reads, ". . . standing out of water and in the water . . ." (KJV). They quote Genesis 1:6-8, which reads, ". . . And God made the firmament, and divided the waters which were under the firmament from the waters which were above the firmament: and it was so." For further support they quote Psalm 104:6-9. They also quote Genesis 2:6, which reads, "but there went up a mist from the earth, and watered the whole face of the ground," along with the appearance of a rainbow after the Flood to prove that rain did not fall until the Flood.

The argument is based translating the word *'erets* as "earth" in Genesis 2:6 because *'erets* is translated "earth" in Genesis 1:1, which reads ". . . God created the heavens and the earth." Therefore, the reference to "earth" in Genesis 2:6 must mean the whole planet.

Several problems are found with the canopy theory. Many plants and animals living today could not survive in the type of climate created by the canopy. That arctic animals, such as polar bears, musk oxen, and walrus, could survive for long in a subtropical climate is questionable.

If unbroken, dense clouds surrounded the Earth, then the amount of sunlight reaching the Earth's surface would be noticeably less than it presently is. Some plants living today would have difficulty surviving under such reduced light. Did these plants evolve after the Flood? The watering mechanism under the canopy theory suggests that much of the vegetation growing on Earth then differs from that growing on Earth now. Except for plants adjacent to streams or bodies of water or growing where the water table was close to the surface, plants would have to be able to survive in a highly humid atmosphere and with low soil moisture. Such an environment is rare today. Have today's plants evolved from those plants that thrived in such an unusual environment as a humid desert? Advocates of the canopy theory imply that they have, though they would deny such implications.

There are also some scriptural problems with the canopy theory. Psalm 104 indicates that the waters above the firmament are ordinary rain clouds. Psalm 148 denies the canopy theory. In verse four the waters above the heavens are commanded to praise God. The reference is clearly directed to Genesis 1:6, 7. This Psalm was written after the Flood. The author understood that the waters above the heavens still existed. Hence, the waters above the heavens do not refer to a water vapor canopy that was destroyed at the onset of the Flood. Verse five and six of Psalm 148 corroborate this conclusion.

Some select Scriptures can be quoted to support the canopy theory. However, other verses strongly suggest that no canopy existed by the time man arrived on Earth.

8
CONCLUSION

The Bible is a racially oriented book.* It is God's word about and primarily for one racial family—the descendants of Adam, the Aryans. It contains only Adam's genealogy. God created the Adamic, White, or Aryan race for His divine purposes. The Aryan race is to be God's witness and to carry His word to all the peoples and races of the world (Isaiah 43:10-12, 21; Matthew 28:19,20).

Traditionalists, fundamentalists, and conservatives, for the most part, interpret the Scriptures to claim that all the races of men are descended from Adam through Noah. Their theory and interpretation cannot be supported without resorting to evolution, which the Bible emphatically denies. Therefore, their theory and interpretation must be rejected.

God created Adam, who became the father of the Aryan race. He had created the other races of man before the creation of Adam. He placed Adam in the Garden of Eden, which was on the Pamir Plateau. After Adam sinned, God forced him to leave the Garden of Eden.

---

*The Bible is also anti-Semitic. Jesus fervently chastised the Jewish leadership. By definition anyone or anything that condemns Jews for any reason is anti-Semitic. Therefore, Jesus and the Bible are anti-Semitic.

Conclusion

Adam migrated eastward to the Tarim Basin. Here he settled and the Aryan race flourished until the Flood. Here is where the basic elements of civilization were developed and eventually carried to the rest of the world.

Death did not enter the world because of Adam's sin. It existed before Adam sinned. Death came to the Aryan race as result of Adam's sin.

After Cain left the Tarim Basin, he settled in Nod, which was in western China. Here he married a Turanian, a pre-Adamic race.

The Flood was not universal. It was a regional flood in the Tarim Basin and probably the surrounding areas. It did destroy all the people in the Tarim Basin except Noah and his family. However, it did not destroy all of mankind.

God created Adam, who became the father of God's chosen race, the Adamic, White, or Aryan race. God created the Aryan race to bring forth His chosen nation, Israel, and to take forth His word and teach other men about God and His Son. God chose Israel, a nation of the Aryan race, to receive his revealed word for mankind and to receive His Son, the purpose of Creation. A study of the Scripture and recorded civilization makes it clear that the Aryan race was God's appointed builder of civilization and the carrier of Messianic tidings.

To keep things in proper perspective, let us turn to Carlyle,

> Ah! it is sad, a terrible thing, to see nigh a whole generation of men and women, professing to be cultivated, looking around in a purblind fashion, and finding no God in this universe. I suppose it is a reaction from the reign of cant and hollow pretense, professing to believe what in fact they do not believe. And this is what we have got to. All

things from frog-spawn; the gospel of dirt the order of the day. The older I grow—and I now stand on the brink of eternity—the more comes back to me the sentence in the catechism which I learned when a child, and the fuller and deeper it becomes: "what is the chief end of man? To glorify God, and enjoy him forever." No gospel of dirt, teaching that men have descended from frogs, through monkeys, can ever set aside.*

---

*[William H. Campbell], *Anthropology for the People: A refutation of the Theory of the Adamic Origin of All Races* (Richmond, 1891) p. 89.

APPENDICES

Appendix 1. Chronology

The following chronology is an approximate estimation. There is no unanimous consensus on many of these dates.

CHRONOLOGY

BP

15 billion	–Universe created
4.5 billion	–Earth formed
120,000	–Riss glaciation ends, Riss-Würm interglacial period begins
75,000	–Australians and Khoisans created
71,000	–Würm I (Phase I of Würm) glaciation begins
62,000	–Würm I glaciation peaks
57,000	–Würm I glaciation ends, Laufen interglacial period (first Würm interstadial) begins
55,000	–Negroes, Turanians, and Melanochroi created
52,000	–Eskimo Turanians appear in northern Farther India
50,000	–Würm II (Phase II of Würm) glaciation begins
	–Dravidian Melanochroi drive Negroes from India

49,000	–Min Turanians appear in Min River Valley of Szechwan
45,000	–Würm II glaciation peaks –Australians spread across East Indies into New Guinea
40,000	–Australians reach Borneo –Negroes arrive in Africa
38,000	–Upper Paleolithic Age begins –Melanochroi enter northern Africa
36,000	–Mins have spread over much of eastern China
35,000	–Würm II glaciation ends, final interglacial period (final Würm interstadial) begins –Neanderthal man becomes extinct –Melanochroi (Grimaldi race) enter Europe from North Africa and bring Aurignacian culture –Dravidians begin to reoccupy Indus River Valley –Eskimos settle along Wei River in Shensi –Turanians move to Tibetan highlands
32,000	–Ugrian Turanians leave Tibetan highlands and settle in Kansu
30,000	–Australians first enter Australia
29,000	–Tunguses migrate to headwaters of Yangtze River
28,000	–Würm III (Phase III of Würm) glaciation (Achen glaciation) begins
27,000	–Paraoean Turanians move from Farther India to upper valleys of Brahmaputra to Yangtze Rivers
25,000	–Würm III glaciation peaks

	–Dravidians invade Deccan and drive out most Pre-Dravidians
	–Tunguses remaining in Tsinghai come down Hwang River and push Ugrians from Kansu to Altai Mountains and Eskimos from Shensi province to Khingan Mountain
24,000	–Dravidians drive most Negroes from Farther India
	–Dravidians reach Yunnan
23,000	–Cro-Magnard Melanochroi migrate across North Africa into Europe
22,000	–Mins enter Alaska
20,000	–Eskimos settle Khingan Mountains
	–Melanochroi (Brünn race) enter Europe from Asia and establish Solutrean culture
	–Mins reach Peruvian Andes
17,000	–Mins and Tunguses enter North America
16,000	–Cro-Magnards establish Magdalenian culture
15,000	–Saharan-Hamites settle in northern Africa

BC

9000	–Australians remaining in Indonesia migrate to Australia
8100	–Adam and Aryans are created
8000	–Würm II glaciation ends
	–Cain banished to Nod and establishes Cainite empire
	–Neolithic Age (New Stone Age) begins
	–Turks expand into western Tibet and Tarim Basin
	–Paraoeans migrate into Burma and Laos
	–Negroes beyond Timbuktu

7800	–Aryans settle in Western Turkestan –Finns migrate to Altai Mountains –Turks enter Pamir and Hindu Kush
7700	–Nordics settle south of Lake Balkhash –Paleo-Celts enter Europe –Ugrians enter North America
7600	–Pre-Sumerian Aryans cross Iranian Plateau, enter Lower Mesopotamia, establish a colony in Elam, and introduce Neolithic culture in Middle East –Indo-Iranian Melanochroi enter India –Dravidians drive nearly all remaining Negroes from Farther India
7500	–Mediterranean Pelasgians enter Balkans and introduce Neolithic culture –Paleo-Celts known as Furfooz-Grenelle people reach North Sea
7000	–Mediterranean Ligurians enter Italy and introduce Neolithic culture –Melanesian Negroes drive Australians from New Guinea to Australia
6500	–Melanochroi develop Caspin culture in northern Africa –Eastern–Hamite Melanochroi enter Ethiopia –Ligurians enter France and Germany and introduce Neolithic culture
6000	–Iberians cross Gaul into Britain –Eastern-Hamites move into Upper Egypt and soon invade Lower Egypt and drive Mediterraneans to Crete
5000	–Eastern-Hamites have spread over Ethiopian highlands and into Somaliland
4300	–Nordics spread across Kirghiz Steppe

Appendices

3500	–Sumerians arrive in Lower Mesopotamia
	–Eastern-Hamite Canaanites settle in Palestine
3300	–Noahic Flood occurs
3200	–descendants of Noah arrive in Middle East, settle along Persian Gulf, and bring writing and bronze
	–Mizraim settle in Egypt
3100	–Upper and Lower Egypt united
3100	–Protodynastic era of Egypt (1st and 2nd Dynasties) begins with beginning of reign of Menes, founder of First Dynasty of Egypt
3000	–Iranian colonies in northern India
	–Dravidians settle in Indonesia
	–Eskimos enter North America
	–Chinese come down Hwang River and take possession of central China
	–Erech built
	–Ninevah founded
	–advent of Greek civilization
	–advent of Minoan civilization
2900	–large number of Negroes taken to Egypt as slaves
	–Early Minoan period of Crete begins
2850	–Chaldeans conquer Sumer and Akkad and establish First Dynasty of Ur
2800	–Akkadians settle in Upper Mesopotamia
2755	–Protodynastic era of Egypt ends; Old Kingdom of Egypt (3rd through 6th Dynasties) begins
2700	–Early Helladic period of Greece begins
2680	–Fourth Dynasty of Egypt, era of pyramid building begins

2680	–reign of Snefru, first king of Fourth Dynasty, builder of first pyramid, begins
2650	–Gilgamesh (Nimrod)
2640	–reign of Snefru ends; reign of Khufu, second king of Fourth Dynasty, builder of the Great Pyramid, begins
2610	–reign of Khufu ends
2544	–Fourth Dynasty of Egypt ends
2500	–Cretans become a major power –Phoenicians settle the coast of Lebanon
2450	–Akkadians conquer Sumer, First Dynasty of Ur collapses, Akkadian Empire is established
2400	–Akkadians found Indus civilization
2300	–Aryan Hittites and Celto–Slavs leave Western Turkestan –Melanochroi fleeing Hittites enter India –Hittites enter Anatolia –Celto-Slavs enter Ukraine –Neo-Celts enter Central Europe –Nordic Suebi enter eastern Europe –Early Bronze Age begins in Europe
2270	–Gutians overthrow Akkadian empire
2255	–Old Kingdom of Egypt ends
2254	–First Intermediate Period of Egypt (7th through 11th Dynasties)
2200	–Neo-Celts settle in Sweden –Hurrians begin overrunning northern Mesopotamia and Syria –Suebians conquered Ukraine
2145	–Gutian rule of Sumer and Akkad collapses
2140	–Chaldeans establish Third Dynasty of Ur
2134	–First Intermediate Period of Egypt ends; Middle Kingdom of Egypt begins

2100   –Early Minoan Period ends and Middle Minoan Period begins on Crete
2050   –Hebrews settle near Ur
2030   –Sumerians overthrow Third Dynasty of Ur
2000   –Hebrews migrate to Padan-Aram
           –Neo-Celts arrive in Skäne
           –Deutro-Malay Turanians began settling Indonesia
1900   –Amorites conquer Babylonia

As illustrated in the following table, unanimous agreement on the creation of Adam and the occurrence of the Flood is absent. The early Church fathers used the Septuagint Scripture and arrived at much earlier dates for the creation of Adam and the Flood than the Church scholars of the Middle Ages and Reformation, who used the Masorete Scriptures. Many recent scholars disregard the Biblical genealogies on the grounds that they are incomplete and arrive at even earlier dates than the early Church fathers.

CREATION OF ADAM AND THE FLOOD

SOURCE	CREATION OF ADAM (B.C.)	FLOOD (B.C.)
Septuagint computation	5586	3246
Septuagint Alexandrinus	5508	
Septuagint Vatican	5270	

SOURCE	CREATION OF ADAM (B.C.)	FLOOD (B.C.)
Samaritan computation	4427	2998
Samaritan text	4305	
Hebrew text	4161	2288
English Bible	4004	2348
Josephus, Universal History	4698	3146
Talmudists	5344 to 3761	
Jewish computation	4220 to 4184	
Vulgar Jewish computation	3760	2104
Clemens Alexandrinus	5624	3476
Hales	5411	3155
Origen	4830	3174
Usher	4004	2348
Calmet	4004	2344
Luther	3961	
Scaliger	3950	2294

SOURCE	CREATION OF ADAM (B.C.)	FLOOD (B.C.)
Suidas	6000	3758
Nicephorus	5500	3258
Eusebius	5200	2958
St. Jerome	3952	2296
Hilarion	5475	3218
St. Julian, LXX	5205	2963
St. Isidore	5336	3094
Montanus	3849	2193
Vossius	5590	3334
Petavius	3983	2327
Theophilus	5529	3287
Julius Africans	5531	3269
Calvin	3,944	
Sumerian records	3,100	
Patten, earlier work		2800
Patten, revised work		2500

SOURCE	CREATION OF ADAM (B.C.)	FLOOD (B.C.)
Haberman		2344
Whitcomb & Morris		5000 to 7000
Dunham	4,041	
Urguhart	8,167	
Orr	12,000 to 15,000	
Unger	8000 to 10,000	5000
Noorbergen		3398
Bunsen	18,000	8000

The following table gives a typical geological time line. Various authorities give different dates.

TYPICAL GEOLOGICAL TIME CHART
(years before the present time)

Pre-Cambrian
    Archeozoic and
        Protozoic   4,650,000,000-600,000,000

Paleozoic
    Cambrian   600,000,000-500,000,000
    Ordovician   500,000,000-435,000,000
    Silurian   435,000,000-400,000,000
    Devonian   400,000,000-345,000,000
    Carboniferous
        Mississippian   345,000,000-310,000,000
        Pennsylvanian   310,000.000-280,000,000
    Permian   280,000,000-230,000,000
Mesozoic
    Triassic   230,000,000-195,000.000
    Jurassic   195,000,000-140,000,000
    Cretaceous   142,000,000-65,000,000
Cenozoic
    Tertiary   65,000,000-2,000,000
    Quaternary   2,000,000 to date

The following table summarizes Patten's catastrophic and galactogenetic time chart.*

PATTEN'S CATASTROPHIC AND GALACTOGENETIC TIME CHART
(B.C.)

I. Pre-Solar Time
    A. Pre-Lunar Time   date of origin-1,000,000,000
       (preceding
       capture of
       Moon)

---

*A detail chart is found on pages 302 to 304 in *The Biblical Flood and the Ice Epoch* by Donald Wesley Patten.

    B. Post-Lunar Time   1,000,000,000-10,000,000
       (movement
       toward Sun's
       domain)
II. Intra-solar Time
    A. Outer-Solar Time
       (Earth-moon
       move within
       Sun's domain)
       1. Invisible Earth   10,000,000-100,100
          (Earth-Moon
          beyond Pluto's
          orbit but within
          Sun's domain)
       2. Visible Era   100,100-100,000
          (Earth-Moon near
          Pluto's orbit)
    B. Inner-Solar Time
       1. Pre-Hydrocarboniferous Era 100,000-20,000
          (Earth warms, ice melts,
          oceans fill, climate
          organized—this and
          previous era correspond
          to pre-Cambrian)
       2. Hydrocarboniferous
          Catastrophic Era   20,000-10,000
          (Appalachian-
          Caledonian-Herzynian
          formed, first life forms
          created—corresponds
          to Paleozoic)

3. Carboniferous Interlude   10,000-2,800
   (canopy develops,
   greenhouse effect, most
   life forms created)
4. Floodtide Catastrophe   2,800
   (Alpine-Himalayan and
   Circum-Pacific orogenetic
   uplift, ice caps formed,
   Noahic flood, fossils formed
   —corresponds to Mesozoic
   and Cenozoic)

Appendix 2. Tarim Basin

The Tarim Basin is in Eastern Turkestan, which is also known as Chinese Turkestan and Kashgaria. This basin lies in the heart of the Asian continent. Much of it is a trackless, desolate desert where rain rarely falls. It is a land of oases and desert where rainfall is less than four inches per year.

Mighty mountain ranges enclose the Tarim Basin on three sides. It is bounded on the northern rim by the high mountain range of the Tien Shan (Heavenly Mountains) whose Bogdo Ula, Barkul, and Karlyk ranges merge into the Nan Shan on the east. On the south it is bounded by the Altyn Tagh, Kunlun (Kuen Lun), and Karakoram mountain systems. The Pamirs are on the west. These mountain ranges that enclose East Turkestan are among the loftiest and most difficult in the world and reach heights of over 20,000 feet.

Eastern Turkestan is an elevated plateau surrounded by high mountains except on the east side. The east side is crumbling remains of a once mighty mountain system. Beyond the eastern boundary lies stretches of barren plateau. The Tarim Basin is 850 miles long and 350 miles wide. At the bottom of the basin is the Taklamakan Desert. From the south, west, and north flow the Aksu, Kara Kash, Yarkand, and other rivers to form the Tarim River. The Tarim River skirts the Taklamakan on the west and north, where it is 4000 feet above sea level. It joins with the Kunche Darya and descends 1,500 feet down to Lop Nor at the eastern end of the desert and empties into the lakes and marshes there.

In the eastern part of the Tarim Basin, north of the Kurugh Tagh and South of the Bogdo Ula, lies the Turfan Basin. It is more than 500 feet below sea level.

Surrounded by mountain ranges, the Tarim Basin of Eastern Turkestan is one of the most desolate places on earth. Today people are able to live there because of water supplied by melting snow caps of the surrounding mountains. Until recently this land has been difficult to reach, and even today access is not easy.

Appendix 3. Early Man and the Stone Age

The stone age of prehistoric times is divided into two ages: Paleolithic or Old Stone Age and Neolithic or New Stone Age.

The Paleolithic Age begins when man or humanoids first began to use stone tools. However, most technological advances occurred during this age after the arrival of the Negro, Turanian, and Melanochroic species of men. During this age the chief implements of man were usually made of stone. His tools were mainly roughly shaped flints. Bones, horns, tusks, and other like materials were also used. Paleolithic man was a hunter and fisherman. He developed the bow and arrow. He was ignorant of the arts of spinning and weaving and knew little of the art of pottery. Except perhaps for the dog, he had no domestic animals. Caves or crude shelters were his dwellings. He built no monuments and did not bury his dead. He knew the use of fire, but probably lacked the knowledge of starting a fire. When the White man first discovered the Australians, he found them in the Paleolithic stage of culture.

The Neolithic Age begins with the creation of the Aryans about 8,100 B.C. During the Neolithic Age stone implements were ground and polished. The weapons and tools were ground to a sharp edge. Axes had handles, which made them a more effective tool. Neolithic man learned to domesticate plants and till the soil. He also domesticated various wild animals. He acquired the knowledge of spinning and weaving and of making fine pottery. Although he sometimes lived in caves, he built houses in which to live. He also built monuments, i.e., monoliths and megaliths. His dead he buried in such a manner to show that he believed in a future life. His religious ideas were well developed. When Columbus discovered America, the Indians were living in a Neolithic culture.

Appendix 4. The Species of Men

Six species of men are extant. These are the Khoisans, Australians, Negroes, Melanochroi, Turanians, and Aryans. Khoisans live mostly in southwest Africa and include the Hottentots and Bushmen. Australians include the Australians of Australia, the Pre-Dravidians of India, and several tribes in Malaysia and Indonesia. Among the Pre-Dravidians are the Veddas, Kolarians, and Sakai. Negroes include the Sudanese, Negrillos, Bantus, Nilotes, and Nilo-Hamites in Africa and the Negritos and Melanesians in Asia and Oceania. Negroes of North and South America are also of this species. Turanians include the Paleosiberians, Tungus, Sinicus (or Chinese), Mins, Paraoeans (or Paleomongolians), Turks, Ugrians, Ainus, Malays, and Indians of America. Melanochroi include the Saharan-Hamites, Eastern-Hamites (or Ethiopians), and Egyptians in Africa; the Orientals (or Southern Arabs) in southwest Asia; and the Dravidians and Indo-Iranians in India and Pakistan. Aryans include the Nordics, East Baltics, Alpines, Mediterraneans, Dinarics, Armenians, Northern Hamites (Berbers of northern Maghreb), Pamiri, Iranians, and Indo-Afghans and their descendants in North and South America, South Africa, and Australia.

Appendix 5. Early Rulers of Egypt

The first six dynasties of Egypt were of the Aryan or White race. The statues and paintings of the kings and ruling class of the "pyramid dynasties" reveal features of the White European race. A portrait of Prince Khufu-Kaf (c. 2650 B.C.), son of King Khufu, builder of the Great Pyramid, had the facial characteristics of a European. Clephren (Khefre), builder of the Second Pyramid (c. 2565 B.C.) also had the physiognomy of a European. The darker races are depicted as slaves. Serological and DNA analysis of Egyptian mummies and skeletons show that the ancient Egyptian rulers were Aryans. To these Aryans goes the credit for the sudden development of Egypt's high civilization.

When the Aryan Mizraim arrived in Egypt, they found it mostly inhabited by the Melanochroic Egyptians, a non-Adamic people akin to the Eastern-Hamites. (Mediterranean Aryans also inhabit Egypt, but in much lesser numbers.) These people they soon subjected to their rule. Thus, Egypt became inhabited by two races, the Mizraim and the Egyptians. The Mizraim were descendants of Ham and racial kinsmen of the Shemites and Israelites. These were the Egyptians whom the Israelites were allowed to marry. The Melanochroic Egyptians were a brown-skinned people, who were related to the Eastern-Hamites. The Egyptians may have also included a hybrid people, a cross between the descendants of Cush and Eastern-Hamites and Egyptians.

Thus, the Hebrews recognized two types of Egyptians: the Mizraim and the Pathrusim. The Mizraim were a Mediterranean Aryan people who mostly inhabited Lower Egypt. The Pathrusim were a Hamitic Melanochroic people who mostly inhabited Upper Egypt,

Pathros, although they comprised a large part of the population in Lower Egypt also. These Pathrusim are the ancestors of today's Egyptian Fellahs.

Appendix 6. Ancient Peoples of Palestine

The Bible identifies several aboriginal people living in Palestine before the descendants of Noah arrived. They included the Anakim, Avvim (Avim), Emim, Horim (Horites), Nephilim, Rephaim, and Zamzummim (Zuzim).

The Anakim are referred to in Numbers 13:22, 28, 33; Deuteronomy 1:28; 2:10, 11, 21; 9:2; Joshua 11:21, 22; 14:12, 15; 15:14; and Judges 1:10, 20. Their name meant "long-necked ones." A tall stalwart people, they were allied or related to the Rephaim. They were descended from the Nephilim. The best-known Anakim was Goliath of Gath, whom David slew, and Anak, who was their progenitor and founder of Kirjath-arba (Hebron). They dwelt in the southern part of Canaan in the Negeb area. They consisted of three tribes: Sheshai, Ahiman, and Talmai. The Israelites under Joshua conquered much of their land. Caleb drove them from Hebron, their chief city. Debir and Anab were other important cities of the Anakim. After being driven from their land by the Israelites, they essentially vanished from history although a remnant was left in Philistine at Gaza, Gath, and Ashdod for sometime afterwards.

The Avvim are referred to in Deuteronomy 2:23 and Joshua 13:3; 18:23. Their name meant "ruins" or "dwellers in ruins." They lived about Gaza in villages in the southern part of the Shefelah, or the foothills, between of the Philistine plains and the mountains of Judah. When the Philistines (Caphtorim) conquered the southern coastline of Palestine shortly after 1200 B.C., they destroyed all but a small remnant of these people. This remnant may have been driven northward to the area around the town of Avim (Joshua 18:23). When the

Israelites arrived in Palestine, the Avvim were living a nomadic life.

The Emim are referred to in Genesis 14:5 and Deuteronomy 2:10, 11. Their name meant "terrible men" or "dreadful ones." Probably related to the Anakim and Rephaim, they were a tall people, as tall as the Anakim. They lived in the land east of the Jordan that the Moabites later occupied. Until Chedorlaomer, king of Elam, defeated them in the plains of Kiriathaim, they were a powerful nation. The Moabites later drove the Emim from their land.

The Horim are referred to in Genesis 14:6, 36:20, 21, 29; and Deuteronomy 2:12, 22. Carving their dwellings out of sheer rock, they were cave dwellers of Mount Seir. They were probably allied with the Rephaim and Emim. Chedorlaomer, king of Elam, defeated and conquered them in the mountainous district of Seir near El-Paran. About 1407 B.C. the Edomites eventually destroyed them. Some believe that the Horites were the Hurrians and not cave dwellers although others dispute this claim. Some believe that they were the Hivites of Joshua's day.

The Nephilim are referred to in Genesis 6:4 and Numbers 13:33. Their name meant "the fallen ones." In Numbers 13:33 they were called the sons of Anak. A people of uncontrollable hatred and violence were the Nephilim. Because of their violent nature, they were often as much of a threat to themselves as others. They are credited with introducing cannibalism into the world. This race existed before and after the Flood. Some believe them to be giant demigods who were the result of the sexual union of the "daughters of men" (mortal women) and the "sons of God" (angels).* Regardless of their origin, they were a tall people with a fierce disposition and debased character. They inhabited southern Canaan. Under the command of Joshua, the Israelites killed or drove them out of the promised land. The Nephilim and Anakim were closely related.

(The common belief is that the Nephilim were the product of the union of the "sons of God" and the "daughters of man." They were not. According to Genesis 6:4, "The Nephilim were in the earth in those days and also after that, when the sons of God came unto the daughters man, and they bare children to them. . . ." This verse states that the Nephilim were living on Earth at the time the sons of God took the daughters of man. As this verse is part of the introduction leading to the Flood, the phrase "also after that" affirms that the Nephilim lived after the Flood. This conclusion is supported by Numbers 13:33 where the Israelite spies saw the Nephilim in Palestine some centuries after the Flood.

If the Nephilim were the prodigy of fallen angels and Adamic women, then either they survived the Flood or the fallen angels again married Adamic women after the Flood. In the days of Moses (Numbers 13:33) lived the Nephilim. With the phrase "and also after that," Genesis 6:4 alludes to their existence at the time of Moses. The text in Genesis 6:4 appears to be using the existence of the Nephilim to mark the time when this

---

*According to the Book of Enoch, Samjaza, or Satan, led a ban of angels to Earth. They saw the beauty of the daughters of man. They lusted after them and took them as wives. Then they taught their wives magic and witchcraft. From this union of fallen angels and women came the Nephilim.

hideous miscegenation occurred. This verse claims that the Nephilim lived before the sons of God married the daughters of man. The Nephilim were renowned at the time of this sin of miscegenation occurred.)

The Rephaim are referred to in Genesis 14:5; 15:20; Deuteronomy 2:11, 20; 3:11, 13; and Joshua 12:4; 13:12; 17:15. Their name meant "ghost or weak," "spirit of the deceased," "lofty men," or "giant aborigines." They were a people of large statue and were probably related to the Emim and Zamzummim. They dwelt along the Jordan and the highlands of Bashan. About 1950 B.C.* Chedorlaomer, king of Elam, conquered them at Ashteroth Karnaim. Before the Israelites arrived, the Moabites and Ammonites had taken much of the Rephaim's land. By the time of the Israelite arrival, the Amorites had absorbed most of the Rephaim. Og, king of Bashan, was one of the last of this nation.† Later the Israelites drove them from Palestine. A remnant appeared to have fled to Philistia.

The Zamzummim are referred to in Genesis 14:5 and Deuteronomy 2:20. Their name meant "noisemakers," "murmurers," "stammerers"—hence, speakers of a barbarous tongue. A tall people, the Zamzummim were closely related to the Rephaim and may have been a tribe of the Rephaim. They inhabited the land east of Jordan

---

*Alternative dates of 2091 B.C. and 1918 B.C. are also given for Chedorlaomer's conquest of the Rephaim.

†Some believe that Og was not of the same nation as that mentioned in Genesis.

until displaced by the Ammonites. Chedorlaomer, king of Elam, conquered them before the arrival of the Ammonites.

Appendix 7. Laws of Nature

The Bible teaches that the laws of nature are the laws of God. It teaches that the regularity of nature is the constancy of God. The uniformity of nature is scriptural. This concept existed long before modern science. For example, in Genesis 8:22, God promises, "While the earth remaineth, seedtime and harvest, and cold and heat, and summer and winter, and day and night shall not cease." In Jeremiah 5:24 God's promise is constancy of rain and harvest time: ". . . Let us now fear Jehovah our God, that giveth rain, both the former and the latter, in its season, that preserveth unto us the appointed weeks of harvest." According to Jeremiah 31:35-36, the Sun, Moon, and stars fulfill their function because they obey the laws by which God controls them: "Thus saith Jehovah, who giveth the sun for a light by day, and the ordinances of the moon and of the stars for a light by night, who stirreth up the sea so that the waves thereof roar; Jehovah of host is his name: If these ordinances depart from before me, saith Jehovah, then the seed of Israel also shall cease from being a nation before me for ever." In Jeremiah 33:20 God proclaims the regularity of night and day a covenant: "Thus saith Jehovah: If ye can break my covenant of the day, and my covenant of the night, so that there shall not be day and night in their season." According to Psalm 148, the Sun, Moon, stars, heavens, and waters above the heavens were established forever and are under a decree that shall not pass away. Many other examples of scriptural teaching that the regularity of nature is a result of God's will can be cited. They include Job 28:26 (rain and lighting), Job 38:8-11, Proverbs 8:29, and Jeremiah 5:22 (oceans), and Psalm 104:8-9 (mountains). The Scriptures affirm the regularity of nature.

Appendix 8. Law of Faunal Succession

The law of faunal succession states that in general the relative age of a given layer of fossil-bearing sedimentary rock can be determined from the fossilized plants and animals contained in it. Younger sedimentary rocks generally contain more complex types of fossilized plants and animals than older rocks. When the layer of sediment was deposited, certain types of living organisms inhabited the Earth. When these organisms died, they became part of the sediment. When a later layer was being deposited, a different population of organisms inhabited the Earth. The population of organisms changed through time. However, the change in populations does not mean that the same species did not live during both periods. This law does not validate the general theory of organic evolution. It merely claims that the overall assemblage or association of species change over time.

Appendix 9. Adam's First Wife

According to Jewish folklore, Eve was not the first woman or the first wife of Adam. Before Eve, Adam had a wife named Lilith. Consumed by her pride, Lilith refused to let Adam lie on top when they had sexual intercourse. Because of this act, she became the patron goddess of the lesbians. She eventually left Adam and migrated to the shores of the Red Sea. Here she indulged in her sexual fantasies.

Lilith acquired the reputation of sucking the life out of newborn children. She was also believed to suck the blood out of men who slept alone—thus her identification as a vampire. In the Bible she is called "the night hag" in Isaiah 34:14, Revised Standard Version translation (the King James translation refers to her in this verse as "screech owl").

Appendix 10. Geocentric Universe

There was a time when the Church held that the Earth was the center of the solar system and the Universe. The Sun, planets, and stars revolved around the Earth. To believe otherwise was to be a heretic. To believe otherwise was tantamount to claiming that the Scriptures were not Divinely inspired.

Although the Scriptures do not specifically claim that the Earth is the center of the Universe, it does describe the Universe from an Earth perspective. Such description can lead a person who is ignorant in astronomy to conclude that the Earth is the center of the Universe.

Passages used by the Church to support its geocentric doctrine included:
1. Psalm 104:5 ("He founded the earth upon its bases, that it should not be moved for ever."—alternative translation.)
2. Psalm 24:2 ("For he hath founded it [the world] upon the seas, And established [or, fixed] it upon the floods [or, streams].")
3. Psalm 136:6 ("To him that spread forth the earth above the water. . . .")
4. Ecclesiastes 1:4, 5 ("One generation goeth, and another generation cometh; but the earth abideth for ever. The sun also ariseth, and the sun goeth down, and hasten to its place where it ariseth.")
5. Psalm 19:5, 6 (". . . [the Sun] rejoiceth as a strong man to run his course. His [the Sun's] going forth is from the end of the heavens, And his circuit unto the ends of it [or, to their uttermost parts]. . . .")

6. Psalm 148:4 ("Praise him, ye heavens of heavens, And ye waters that are above the heavens.")
7. Psalm 104:2, 3 (. . . Who stretchest out the heavens like a curtain; Who layeth the beams of his chambers in the water. . . .")

Based upon these and related passages, the Church held that the Sun moved around the Earth every 24 hours. The Earth rested immoveable at the center of the Universe. Because it was founded and fixed upon pillars, bases, and pedestals, the Earth could not possibly move.

One great mistake that the Church made in interpreting these passages is to interpret them too literally. Poetry expresses feelings and concepts. It uses words to paint pictures. The words should not be construed too literally. However, the major mistake was to use Scripture to defend orthodox science, which then favored a geocentric universe.

Many Biblical passages describe the Earth as flat, supported by pillars, surrounded by water, and covered by a solid dome. A literal interpretation would lead one to believe that either the Bible is false, and therefore, not inspired, or the facts of science are false. The writers of these passages are describing the Universe from an earthly perspective of a layman and not with a scientific perspective.

The following verses depict the Earth as round and flat and supported on pillars:
1. Job 9:6 ("That shaketh the earth out of its place, And the pillars thereof tremble.")
2. 1 Samuel 2:8 (". . . For the pillars of the earth are Jehovah's, And he hath set the world upon them.")

Appendices

3. Psalm 104:5 ("Who laid the foundation of the earth [or, He founded the earth upon its bases], that it should not be moved for ever.")

The following verses depict the earth as covered by a solid dome of the firmament supported by mountain-pillars:

1. Job 26:11 ("The pillars of heaven tremble And are astonished at his rebuke.")
2. Job 37:18 ("Canst thou with him spread out the sky, Which is strong as a molten mirror?")

The following verses depict the earth as surrounded by water:

1. Genesis 1:6, 7 ("And God said, Let there be a firmament in the midst of the waters, and let it divide the waters from the waters. And God made the firmament, and divided the waters which were under the firmament from the waters which were above the firmament: and it was so.")
2. Genesis 7:11 (". . . were all the fountains of the great deep broken up, and the windows of heaven opened.")
3. Genesis 8:2 ("the fountains also of the deep and the windows of heaven were stopped. . . .")
4. Psalm 24:2 ("For he hath founded it [the Earth] upon the seas, And established it upon the floods.")
5. Psalm 148:4 ("Praise him . . . ye waters that are above the heavens.)

The following verses depict the Sun, Moon, and stars as fixed or moving across the firmament:

1. Psalm 19:4, 6 ("Their line is gone out through all the earth, and their words to the end of the

world. In them hath he set a tabernacle for the sun, . . . His going forth is from the end of the heavens, and his circuit unto the ends of it; and there is nothing hid from the heat thereof.")

As these passages show the theory that the Earth is flat, supported by pillars, surrounded by water, and covered by a solid dome is easily supported by Scripture. The Bible supports this theory as well as, if not better than, the theories of creation in six 24-hour days, a universal flood, or Adam as the father of all races of men.

Anyone who defends creation in six 24-hour days or a universal flood, or even the concept that all the races of men descended from Adam or Noah because of a strict literal reading of the Bible supports such interpretation, needs to defend the theory of a flat Earth supported on pillars, covered by a solid dome, and surrounded completely by water. If he is consistent, he needs to defend the theory of a geocentric universe.

Appendix 11. Create

"Create" is the translation of the Hebrew word *bârâ* (Strong O.T. #1254). Three times it is used in Genesis One. It is used for the heavens and Earth, i.e., the Universe. It is used for sea creatures and birds, i.e., animal life, on the fifth day. Finally, it is used for man (Adam).

Bârâ implies a miraculous act, the origin of something entirely new, e.g., the Universe, life, or Adamic man, that did not exist before. It means more than just making something new out of existing material. It is the original creation of existing materials, the creation of something out of nothing. It is the creation of something new or the addition of a new thing to a new arrangement of existing material. For example, God added life-force to animal bodies made of existing material. He added that substance to the body of man that made Adam the image of God.* In the Bible only God is used as the subject of *bârâ*, for only God can create in the sense inferred in *bârâ*.

---

*This new substance was the very breath of God that became Adam's spirit. Other animals and races of men became living creatures by other means.

Appendix 12. Man: 'âdâm and îysh

In the Old Testament two words commonly translated man are 'âdâm and îysh. The former always refers to Adam or the Adamic race of man. The latter refers to males or man in general. It usually refers to non-Adamic races, i.e., the pre-Adamites. In many passages 'âdâm and îysh are used to contrast one with the other, that is, to contrast the Aryan race with the other races of men.

For example, Psalm 49:1, 2 reads, "Hear this all ye peoples; Give ear, all ye inhabitants of the world, Both low and high, Rich and poor together." Here "low and high" literally mean sons of Adam ('âdâm) and sons of man (îysh). Again, in Psalm 62:9, "Surely men of low degree are vanity, and men of high degree are a lie. . . ." A literal rendering of this passage would read, "Surely sons of Adam are vanity and sons of man are a lie. . . ."

Other examples can be found in Isaiah. Isaiah 2:9 reads, "And the mean man is bowed down and the great man is brought low. . . ." A literal reading of this passage yields, "And the Adamites boweth down like as man (îysh) humblest himself." Again, in Isaiah 5:15, "And the mean man is bowed down and the great man is humbled. . . ." A literal rendering of this passage is "And the Adamite shall bow down, and the man (îysh) shall humble himself." Isaiah 31:8 shows a similar contrast.

More than seventy times does îysh, or its plural or variation of it, occur in the same sentence with 'âdâm. In some of these passages îysh includes both Adamic and non-Adamic man. This is especially true where male and female are contrasted, e.g., Genesis 2:24. However, in other passages, such as those discussed above, it includes only non-Adamic races of men. The Bible distinguishes between two groups of men: Adam and his descendants, who are the Aryans, and all other races of men. Such distinction strongly suggests, if not emphatically prove, that Adam is not the father of all mankind.

REFERENCES

Albritton, Jr., Claude C., editor. *Philosophy of Geohistory: 1785-1970.* Stroudsburg, Pennsylvania: Dowden, Hutchinson & Ross, Inc. 1975.

Allchin, Bridget and Raymond Allchin. *The Birth of Indian Civilization: India and Pakistan before 500 B.C.* Baltimore, Maryland: Penguin Books Inc., 1968.

Amplified Bible; Containing the Amplified Old Testament and the Amplified New Testament. Grand Rapids, Michigan: Zondervan Publishing House, 1965.

Babun, Edward. *The Varieties of Man: An Introduction to Human Races.* London, England: Crowell-Macmillian Limited, 1969.

Bean, Dr. Robert B. *The Races of Man: Differentiation and Dispersal of Man.* New York, New York: The University Press, 1932.

Berlitz, Charles. *Mysteries from Forgotten Worlds.* New York, New York: Dell Publishing Co., Inc., 1972.

Bevan, J. O. *The Scientific Basis of Religion.* London, England: George Allen & Company, Ltd., 1912.

Bowman, John. *Early Civilization,* I, in *The Universal History of the World.* Irwin Shapiro, editor. New York, New York: Golden Press, 1966.

Branigan, Keith. *The Foundation of Palatial Crete: A Survey of Crete in the Early Bronze Age*. New York, New York: Praeger Publishers, 1970.

Bray, Frank Chapin. *Bray's University Dictionary of Mythology*. New York, New York: Thomas Y. Crowell Company, 1935, Apollo edition 1964.

Breasted, Dr. James H. *A History of Egypt from the Earliest Times to the Persian Conquests*. Second edition. New York, New York: Charles Scriner's Sons, 1937.

Breasted, Dr. James H. *The Conquest of Civilization*. New York, New York: Harper & Brothers Publishers, 1926.

Brinton, Crane, *et al*. *Civilization in the West*. Englewood Cliffs, New Jersey: Prentice-Hall, Inc., 1961.

Bristowe, Mrs. Sydney. *Sargon the Magnificent*. Burnaby, British Columbia: The Association of the Covenant People.

Bristowe, Mrs. Sydney. *The Man Who Built the Great Pyramid*.

[Campbell, William H.] *Anthropology for the People: a Refutation of the Theory of the Adamic Origin of All Races*. Richmond, Virginia: Everett Waddey Co., 1891.

Charroux, Robert. *Forgotten Worlds: Scientific Secrets of the Ancients and Their Warning for Our Time*. Translator Lowell Bair. New York, New York: Popular Library, 1971, 1973.

Charroux, Robert. *Legacy of the Gods*. Translator Berkley Publishing Corporation. New York, New York: Berkley Publishing Corporation, 1965, 1974.

Charroux, Robert. *One Hundred Thousand Years of Man's Unknown History.* Translator Lowell Bair. New York, New York: Berkley Publishing Corporation, 1963, 1970.

Charroux, Robert. *The Gods Unknown.* Translator Neville Spearman. New York, New York: Berkley Publishing Corporation, 1969, 1972.

Chen, Jack. *The Sinkiang Story.* New York, New York: MacMillan Publishing Co. Inc., 1977.

Churchward, James. *The Lost Continent of Mu.* New York, New York: Paperback Library, 1959.

Clarke, W. K. Lowther. *Concise Bible Commentary.* New York, New York: The Macmillian Company, 1953.

Coon, Carleton S. *The Origin of Races.* New York, New York: Alfred A. Knopf, 1962.

Curtin, Philip, *et al. African History.* New York, New York: Longman Inc., 1978.

Davies, G. Henton, Alan Richardson, and Charles L. Wallis, editors. *Twentieth Century Bible Commentary.* Revised edition. New York, New York: Harper & Brothers, Publishers, 1955.

Davis, John D. *A Dictionary of the Bible.* Fourth Revised Edition. Grand Rapids, Michigan: Baker Book House, 1957.

Davis, John D. *The Westminster Dictionary of the Bible.* Revised and rewritten by Henry Snyder Gehman. Philadelphia, Pennsylvania: The Westminster Press, 1944.

Donnelly, Ignatius. *Atlantis: The Antediluvian World.* Revised edition. New York, New York: Gramercy Publishing Company, 1949.

Dummelow, J. R., editor. *A Commentary on the Holy Bible*. New York, New York: Macmillian Publishing Co., Inc., 1936.

Duruy, Victor. *A History of the World*. Volume III, *Ancient History*. Edited and revised by Clement Wood. Cleveland, Ohio: The World Syndicate Publishing Co., 1937.

Eiselen, Frederick Carl, Edwin Lewis, and David G. Downey. *The Abingdon Bible Commentary*. New York, New York: Abingdon-Cokesbury Press, 1929.

Fairservis, Walter A., Jr. *The Roots of Ancient India: The Archaeology of Early Indian Civilization*. New York, New York: The MacMillan Company, 1971.

Fasken, W. H. *Israel's Racial Origin and Migration*. Hollywood, California: New Christian Crusade Church.

Fausset, A. R. *Fausset's Bible Dictionary*. Grand Rapids, Michigan: Zondervan Publishing House, 1949.

Fenton, Ferrar, translator. *The Holy Bible in Modern English*. Merrimac, Massachusetts: Destiny Publishers, 1903. Reprinted 1966.

Ferguson, Wallace K. and Geoffrey Brunn. *A Survey of European Civilization*. Part one: "To 1660." Second edition. Cambridge, Massachusetts: The Riverside Press, 1947.

From the Earliest Times to the Egyptian Empire: 4000-1580 B.C. In *Universal World History*, volume 1. Editor J. A. Hammerton. New York, New York: Wise & Co., 1937.

Garber, Janet S., ed. *The Concise Encyclopedia of Ancient Civilization*. New York, New York: Franklin Watts, 1975.

Garrett, Duane A. *Rethinking Genesis: The Source and Authorship of the First Book of the Pentateuch.* Grand Rapids, Michigan: Baker Book House Company, 1991.

Gaunt, Bonnie. *Beginnings the Sacred Design: A Search for Beginnings, and the Eloquent Design of Creation.* 1995.

Gore, Charles, Henry L. Goudge, and Alfred Guillaume. *A New Commentary on Holy Scripture Including the Apocrypha.* New York, New York: The Macmillian Company, 1928.

Gowlett, John. *Ascent to Civilization.* Editors Louisa McDonnell and Emma Fisher. New York, New York: Alfred A. Knopf, Inc., 1984.

Gribbin, John. *Genesis: The Origins of Man and the Universe.* New York, New York: Delacorte Press/Eleanor Friede, 1981.

Haberman, Frederick. *Tracing Our White Ancestors.* Second edition. Phoenix, Arizona: America's Promise Lord's Covenant Church, 1962, reprinted 1979.

Halley, Henry H. *Halley's Bible Handbook: An Abbreviated Bible Commentary.* 24th edition. Grand Rapids, Michigan: Zondervan Publishing House, 1965.

Harden, Donald. *The Phoenicians.* New York, New York: Frederick A. Praeger, 1962.

Hawking, Stephen W. *A Brief History of Time from the Big Bang to Black Holes.* New York, New York: Bantam Doubleday Dell Publishing Group, Inc., 1988.

Hayes, Carlton J. H. And Parker T. Moon. *Ancient and Medieval History.* New York, New York: The Macmillan Company, 1929.

Henry, Matthew. *Concise Commentary on the Bible*. Chicago, Illinois: Moody Press.

Holy Bible: The New King James Version Containing the Old and New Testaments. Nashville, Tennessee: Thomas Nelson Publishers, 1982.

Holy Scriptures According to the Masoretic Text: A New Translation. Philadelphia, Pennsylvania: The Jewish Publication Society of America, 1917.

Hurlbut, Jesse Lyman. *A Bible Atlas: A Manual of Biblical Geography and History*. New York, New York: Rand McNally and Company, 1938, 1944 edition.

In the Image of God. Merrimac, Massachusetts: Destiny Publishers, 1967.

Jacobus, Melancthon W., Edward E. Nourse, and Andrew C. Zenos. *A New Bible Dictionary*. New York, New York: Funk & Wagnalls Company, 1925.

Jastrow, Morris. *The Civilization of Babylonia and Assyria: Its Remains, Language, History, Religion, Commerce, Law, Art, and Literature*. New York, New York: Benjamin Blom, Inc., 1915 (reissued 1971).

Keane, A. H. *Ethnology*. Cambridge, England: The University Press, 1896.

Kephart, Calvin. *Races of Mankind: Their Origin and Migration*. New York, New York: Philosophical Library, Inc., 1960.

Kramer, Samuel Noah. *The Sumerians: Their History, Culture, and Character*. Chicago, Illinois: The University of Chicago Press, 1963.

Lamsa, George M., translator. *The Holy Bible from Ancient Eastern Manuscripts Containing the Old and New Testaments Translated from the Peshitta, the Authorized Bible of the Church of the East.* Nashville, Tennessee: A. J. Holman Company, 1968.

Langer, William L., editor. *An Encyclopedia of World History.* Boston, Massachusetts: Houghton Miffin Company, 1948.

Lattimore, Owen. *Pivot of Asia: Sinkiang and the Inner Asian Frontiers of China and Russia.* Boston, Massachusetts: Little, Brown and Company, 1950.

Laymon, Charles M., editor. *The Interpreter's One-Volume Commentary on the Bible.* Nashville, Tennessee: Abingdon Press, 1971.

M'Causland, Dominick. *Adam and the Adamite; or, the Harmony of Scripture and Ethnology.* Second edition. London, England: Richard Bentley, 1868.

Maspero, Gaston. *The Dawn of Civilization.* Translated by M. L. McClure. 1894 edition. New York, New York: Frederick Ungar Publishing Co., 1968.

McEvedy, Colin. *The Penguin Atlas of Ancient History.* New York, New York: Penguin Books, 1967.

Megaw, Vincent and Rhys Jones. *The Dawn of Man.* In *The Putnam Pictorial Source Series.* New York, New York: G. P. Putnam's Sons, 1972.

Miller, Madeleine S. and J. Lane Miller. *Harper's Bible Dictionary.* New York, New York: Harper & Brothers, Publishers, 1959.

Moffatt, James. *A New Translation of the Bible Containing the Old and New Testaments*. New York, New York: Harper & Brothers Publishers, 1935.

Mullins, Eustace. *The Curse of Canaan: A Demonology of History*. Stauton, Virginia: Revelation Books, 1987.

Myers, Philip van Ness. *Ancient History*. Second revised edition. Boston, Massachusetts: Ginn and Company, 1916.

Nelson, Byron C. *After Its Kind*. Revised edition. Grand Rapids, Michigan: Baker Book House, 1967.

Nelson, Byron C. *Before Abraham: Prehistoric Man in Biblical Light*. Minneapolis, Minnesota: Augsburg Publishing House, 1948.

Nelson, Byron C. *The Deluge Story in Stone: A History of the Flood Theory of Geology*. Minneapolis, Minnesota: Bethany Fellowship, Inc., 1968.

New American Standard Bible. Reference Edition. Collins World, 1975.

New English Bible. Collins World, 1970.

Noorbergen, Rene. *Secrets of the Lost Races: New Discoveries of Advanced Technology in Ancient Civilizations*. Indianapolis, Indiana: The Bobbs-Merrill Company, Inc., 1977.

Nott, Dr. J. C. And George R. Gliddon. *Types of Mankind: Or, Ethnological Researchers*. 1854; reprint. Miami, Florida: Mnemosyne Publishing Company, Inc., 1969.

Patten, Donald W., et al. *The Long Day of Joshua and Six Other Catastrophes: A Unified Theory of Catastrophism.* Seattle, Washington: Pacific Meridian Publishing Co., 1973.

Patten, Donald W. *The Biblical Flood and the Ice Epoch: A Study in Scientific History.* Seattle, Washington: Pacific Meridian Publishing Co., 1966.

Peake, Arthur S., editor. *A Commentary on the Bible.* New York, New York: Thomas Nelson & Sons.

Pfeiffer, Charles F. and Everett F. Harrison, editors. *The Wycliffe Bible Commentary.* Chicago, Illinois: Moody Press, 1962.

Pieters, Albertus. *Notes on Genesis.* In *Old Testament History*, volume 1. Grand Rapids, Michigan: Wm. B. Eerdmans Publishing Company, 1943.

Platon, Nicolas. *Crete.* Cleveland, Ohio: The World Publishing Company, 1966.

Ramm, Bernard. *The Christian View of Science and Scripture.* Grand Rapids, Michigan: Wm. B. Eerdmans Publishing Company, 1954.

Rand, Howard B. *In the Days of Noah.* Merrimac, Massachusetts: Destiny Publishers.

Ransom, C. J. *The Age of Velikovsky.* New York, New York: Dell Publishing Co., Inc., 1976.

Rawlinson, George. *The Story of Phoenicia.* New York, New York: G. P. Putnam's Sons, 1889.

Robinson, Charles Alexander, Jr. *Ancient History from Prehistoric Times to the Death of Justinian*. New York, New York: The Macmillian Company, 1951.

Ryle, Herbert E. *The Early Narratives of Genesis: A Brief Introduction to the Study of Genesis I.-XI*. New York, New York: The MacMillan Company, 1904.

Saggs, H. W. F. *The Greatness That Was Babylon: A Sketch of the Ancient Civilization of the Tigris-Euphrates Valley*. New York, New York: Hawthorn Books, Inc., 1962.

Saint Joseph "New Catholic Edition" of the Holy Bible. New York, New York: Catholic Book Publishing Company, 1962.

Sanden, D. E. *Does Science Support the Scriptures?* Grand Rapids, Michigan: Zondervan Publishing House, 1951.

Sayce, Archibald H. *Ancient Empires of the East*. Edited by Christopher Johnston. New York, New York: P. F. Collier & Sons Company, 1932.

Sayce, A. A. and R. Peterson. *Race in Ancient Egypt and the Old Testament*. Washington, D.C.: Scott-Townsend Publishers, 1993.

Sendy Jean. *Those Gods Who Made Heaven & Earth: The Novel of the Bible*. Translator Lowell Bair. New York, New York: Berkley Publishing Corporation, 1972.

Scofield, C. I., editor. *The Holy Bible: Scofield Reference Bible*. New and improved edition. New York, New York: Oxford University Press, 1917.

Smith, G. Elliot. *Human History*. New York, New York: W. W. Norton & Company, Inc. 1929.

Smith, J. M. Powis and Edgar J. Goodspeed, translators. *The Complete Bible: An American Translation*. Chicago, Illinois: The University of Chicago Press, 1939.

Smith, John Pye. *The Relation Between the Holy Scriptures and Some Parts of Theological Science*. 5th edition. London: Henry G. Bohn, 1854.

Smith, William. *A Dictionary of the Bible*. Revised and edited by F. N. and M. A. Peloubet. Nashville, Tennessee: Thomas Nelson Publishers, 1979.

Steele, Dr. Joel D. and Esther B. Steele. *A Brief History of Ancient Peoples with Some Account of Their Monuments, Institutions, Arts, Manners, and Customs*. New York, New York: American Book Company, 1881.

Stevens, Sherrill G. *Genesis*. In *Layman's Bible Book Commentary*, volume 1. Nashville, Tennessee: Broadman Press, 1978.

Strong, James. *Strong's Exhaustive Concordance of the Bible with Brief Dictionaries of the Hebrew and Greek Words of the Original with References to the English Words*.

Talbott, Stephen L., ed. *Velikovsky Reconsidered*. New York, New York: Warner Books, 1976,

Tomas, Andrew. *The Home of the Gods: Atlantis from Legend to Discovery*. New York, New York: Berkley Publishing Corp., 1972.

Umland, Craig and Eric Umland. *Mystery of the Ancients: Early Spacemen and the Mayan*. New York, New York: The New American Library, 1974.

Unger, Merrill F. *Archaeology and the Old Testament*. Grand Rapids, Michigan: Zondervan Publishing House, 1954.

Unger, Merrill F. *Unger's Bible Dictionary*. Third edition. Chicago, Illinois: Moody Press, 1960.

Unger, Merrill F. *Unger's Bible Handbook: An Essential Guide to Understanding the Bible*. Chicago, Illinois: Moody Press, 1966.

Velikovsky, Immanuel. *Earth in Upheaval*. New York, New York: Dell Publishing Company., Inc., 1955.

Velikovsky, Immanuel. *Worlds in Collision*. New York, New York: Dell Publishing Company, Inc., 1950.

Verkuyl, Gerrit, editor. *The Holy Bible: The Berkeley Version in Modern English*. Fourth edition. Grand Rapids, Michigan: Zondervan Publishing House, 1960.

Vine, W. E., Merrill F. Unger, and William White, Jr. *Vine's Complete Expository Dictionary of Old and New Testament Words*. Nashville, Tennessee: Thomas Nelson Publishers, 1985.

Waddell, L. A. *Egyptian Civilization: Its Sumerian Origin & Real Chronology & Sumerian Origin of Egyptian Hieroglyphs*. Hawthorne, California: Christian Book Club.

Wallbank, T. Walter, et al. *Civilization, Past and Present*. Third edition. Glenview, Illinois: Scott, Foresman and Company, 1967.

Weisman, Charles A. *The Origin of Race and Civilization as Studied and Verified from Science, History, and the Holy Scriptures*. Third edition. Burnsville, Minnesota: Weisman Publications, 1990.

Wendt, Herbert. *It Began in Babel: The Story of the Birth and Development of Races and Peoples.* Translator James Kirkup. Boston, Massachusetts: Houghton Mifflin Company, 1961.

Whitcomb, John C. and Henry M. Morris. *The Genesis Flood: The Biblical Record and Its Scientific Implications.* Grand Rapids, Michigan: Baker Book House, 1961.

Weymouth, Richard Francis, translator. *New Testament in Modern Speech.* Revised by James Alexander Robertson. Boston, Massachusetts: The Pilgrim Press, 1939.

Wilson, Carl L. and Walter E. Loomis. *Botany.* Third edition. New York, New York: Holt, Rinehart and Winston, 1962.

Worrell, William H. *A Study of Races in the Near East.* Cambridge, England: W. Heffer & Sons Ltd., 1927.

Young, Davis A. *Christianity & the Age of the Earth.* Thousand Oaks, California: Artisan Sales, 1988.

Young, Davis A. *Creation and the Flood: An Alternative to Flood Geology and Theistic Evolution.* Grand Rapids, Michigan: Baker Book House, 1977.

Young Edward J. *Studies in Genesis One.* Philadelphia, Pennsylvania: Presbyterian and Reformed Publishing Co., 1964.

INDEX

Subject Index

Abel, 60, 82, 84
Abraham (see Abram), 64, 116, 132, 152, 153
Abram (see Abraham), 116, 153
Abu Sharem, 73
Adam, 1, 2, 5, 6, 15, 28, 37, 38, 40-42, 51, 58-71, 73, 76-79, 81-83, 97, 127, 129, 133, 157, 161, 162, 171, 192, 196-199
Adamic man, 37, 58, 59, 70, 71, 75, 76, 82, 87, 133-135, 137, 197, 198
Adamic race, 5, 58, 59, 69-71, 76, 81, 83, 137, 162, 198
Adamites, 78, 81, 84, 129, 133, 134, 137, 198
Adapa, 73
Aegean Sea, 91, 140, 141, 150, 151
Aeolians, 140
Afghanistan, 90
Agade, 148

agriculture, 84, 85, 119, 137
Ainus, 182
Akkad, 148, 152, 169, 170
Akkadians, 148
Alans, 140
Alaska, 57, 167
Alexandretta, Gulf of, 150
Algeria, 142
all, 63, 94, 95
Alpines, 149, 157, 177, 182
Alpine-Himalayan cycle of mountains, 157
Alps, 89
Altai Mountains, 86, 88, 167, 168
amebas, 79
America, 57, 94, 95, 103, 123, 124, 130, 167-169, 181, 182
Ammonites, 188, 189
Amorites, 143, 151, 188
amphibians, 37
Amu Darya, 74, 88
Anab, 185
anaesthesia, 11
Anakim, 185-187
Anamim, 142
Anatolia (see Asia Minor), 90, 149, 150, 170

216 Index

Anatolian Plateau, 52, 53
Andes, 57, 115, 167
Andromeda galaxy, 28
angels, 100, 133, 187
animal life, 34, 36, 37, 79, 83, 101, 102, 197
anteaters, 103
anthropoids, 79
antipodes, 11
apparent age, 21
Arabia, 54, 90, 138, 141, 147, 148
Arabian Sea, 54, 56
Aral Sea, 86
Aram, 144, 145, 151, 171
Aramaeans, 145, 151, 152
archaeology, 9
Archeozoic Era, 33, 38, 174
Ark, 94, 96, 102, 103, 105, 109, 116, 119, 120, 126-128, 130, 135, 143
Arkites, 143
armadillos, 102
Armenia, 139
Armenian Highlands, 73
Armenians, 73, 139, 149, 182
Arphaxad, 144, 146
Artaei, 92
Arvadites, 143
Aryans, 1, 3-6, 40, 41, 45-48, 58, 59, 63, 65-68, 70, 71, 76, 77, 82, 84, 86-90, 92, 97, 98, 100, 102, 121, 128, 129, 134, 135, 137, 147-151, 161, 162, 167, 168, 180, 182, 183, 198, 199
Ashdod, 185
Ashkenaz, 139
Ashkenazic Jews, 139
Asia, 53, 57, 71, 74, 84-86, 90, 103, 137, 138, 140, 142, 145, 148, 151, 167, 182
Asia Minor (see Anatolia), 90, 138, 140, 142, 145
Asshur, 144
Assyria, 74, 146, 151, 206
Assyrians, 90, 144, 149, 151
astral catastrophe, 14, 108, 154, 158
astral catastrophe theory, 14, 154, 158
astronomy, 9, 10, 25, 137, 193
Atlantic Ocean, 131
Atlantis, 123, 131
Atlas Mountains, 53
atmosphere, 33, 159
Augustine, 27
Aurignacian culture, 55, 166
Aurora Borealis, 32
Australia, 95, 103, 104, 123, 130, 166-168, 182

Index

Australians, 51-54, 69, 124, 168, 180, 182
Avim, 185
Avvim, 185, 186
Baal, 144
Babylon, 86, 92, 145
Babylonia, 146, 148, 149, 151, 152, 171
Babylonian culture, 86
Babylonian Empire, 146
Babylonian mythology, 32
Bagdad, 148
Balaam, 62, 63
Balak, 62
Balkans, 91, 150, 168
Baltic plains, 89
Baluchistan, 56
Bantus, 182
Barbary, 142
Bashan, 188
Basque, 139
batholiths, 114
Bavaria, 56
beast of the earth, 37, 80, 109
Bel, 146
Berbers, 4, 91, 142, 143, 182
Bible, 1, 2, 5-9, 11, 13-17, 21-23, 27, 49-51, 58, 60-67, 74, 81, 94, 96, 97, 101, 102, 115, 128, 139-145, 147, 155, 161, 172, 185, 190, 192, 194, 196-198

biological laws, 22, 34, 126
biology, 20, 94
birds, 37, 109, 197
Bishop of Ely, 135
Bithynia, 150
Black Sea, 56, 89, 139-141, 149, 150
Blue River, 57
bristle cone pine, 108
British Columbia, 114
British Isles, 89, 150
Bronze Age, 147, 170
Brünn race, 56, 167
bryophytes, 34, 35
Burma, 53, 54, 167
Cain, 58, 60-63, 78, 84-88, 95, 121, 162
Cainite empire, 58, 167
Cainites, 84, 86, 87, 121, 129, 133, 134
Caleb, 185
California, 114
Campbell, William H., 70
Canaan, 100, 116, 141, 143-145, 185, 187
cannibalism, 146, 186
canopy theory, 21, 33-36, 106-108, 131, 157-160, 177
Caphtorim, 142, 185
Cappadocia, 150
carbonate rocks, 110
Carboniferous period, 35, 37, 175, 177
Carlyle, Thomas, 162
carnivores, 78, 79, 81, 105, 126

Carthaginians, 140, 143
Casluhim, 142
Caspian Sea, 55, 56, 86, 89, 139-141, 149
catastrophe, 14, 25, 35, 37, 74, 105, 107, 108, 121, 123, 126, 154-158, 177
Caucasians, 139
Caucasus Mountains, 89, 149
Caucones, 150
Celto-Slavs, 149
Celts, 88, 89, 91, 139, 149, 168, 170, 171
Cenozoic Era, 38, 175, 177
Central Africa, 98
Central Asia, 71, 74, 84-86, 137, 148
Chachmises, 74
Chaldea, 116, 129
Chaldeans, 123, 144, 148, 149
Chambers, Dr., 194
Chedorlaomer, 186, 188, 189
China, 57, 84, 86, 129, 130, 162, 166, 169
Chitral River, 74
Chittim, 140
Chota Plateau, 53
Christ, 11, 64, 65, 71, 121, 126, 136
Christianity, 11, 12, 24, 30, 110, 126
Chudes, 88
Church, 10, 11, 67, 136, 141, 171, 193, 194
Churchward, James, 123
Cilicia, 140
Cimmerians, 88, 89, 139
civilization, 59, 67, 74, 77, 85-87, 92, 116, 117, 121, 122, 129, 131, 137, 162, 169, 170, 183
clastic sediments, 112
Clephren, 183
conscience, 70, 71
conservative theologians, 1, 2, 15, 20
Coon, Carlton S., 42
Copernicus, 10
coral reefs, 110, 113
Cornwall, 150
coyote, 102
create, 37, 132, 197
creation, 5, 7, 8, 12, 13, 16, 18-27, 29-31, 33-41, 48, 50, 52, 58, 59, 61, 67, 68, 76-78, 81-83, 104, 138, 157, 161, 162, 171, 180, 196, 197
creation of man, 40, 59
creation of the Earth, 16, 18, 25
creation of the Universe, 12, 16, 19
creationists, 15, 20-23, 40-43, 46-51, 67, 68, 78-81, 94,

Index

96-99, 103
Cretaceous period, 175
Cretan culture, 92
Cretans, 151
Crete, 92, 140, 142, 168, 169, 171
Crimea, 139
Cro-Magnards, 55, 56
curse of Canaan, 143, 144
Cyprus, 140
Daedalus, 87
Damascus, 153
Danube River, 56, 89, 149
Darada, 74
Dardanians, 140
daughters of man, 100, 133, 134, 187, 188
David, 64, 66, 185
Dawson, Principal, 14
day, 26, 27
Day Age Theory, 24
day of rest, 22, 27, 38, 126
death, 2, 7, 61, 64, 77-82, 162
Debir, 185
Deccan Plateau, 52-54, 167
devil, 11, 124
Devonian period, 35, 175
dew, 107
Dinarics, 182
dinosaur tracks, 112
DNA, 40, 183
Dodanim, 140
dog, 44, 102, 180
Dravidians, 53-56, 86, 167, 182
Earth, 3, 8-13, 16, 18-21, 24-27, 30-33, 36, 37, 39, 58-60, 63, 64, 69, 71, 78, 80, 81, 84, 94-96, 100, 104-110, 114, 120, 121, 123, 126, 129-133, 154-160, 176, 179, 187, 190, 191, 193-197
East Africa, 55
East Asia, 53
East Baltics, 182
East China Sea, 86
East Indies (see Indonesia), 54, 166
Eastern Turkestan, 58, 83, 84, 87, 129, 130, 137, 149, 178, 179
Eastern-Hamites, 56, 92, 148, 182, 183
Eber, 145, 151
Eden, 38, 59, 60, 71-76, 83, 84, 115, 116, 129, 161
edentates, 102, 106
Edomites, 186
egalitarianism, 51
Egypt, 56, 90-92, 94, 116, 117, 129, 137, 141, 142, 148, 151, 168-170, 183, 184
Egyptians, 50, 56, 92, 94, 182, 183
eighth day, 22

Elam, 90, 144-147, 168, 186, 188, 189
Elamites, 90, 146, 148
Elishah, 140
Emim, 185, 186, 188
energy, 17, 18, 23, 31, 146
England, 91
Enoch, 62, 63, 84, 85, 87, 187
Enosh Catastrophe, 157
eolian deserts, 113
equality, 2, 43, 46, 51
Erech, 85
Eridu, 73, 92
eternity, 69
ethics, 7
Etruscans, 140, 141
Euphrates River, 72-74, 115, 145, 152
Eurasia, 40, 87
Europe, 53, 55, 56, 85, 89, 91, 100, 103, 117, 139, 149, 150, 166-168, 170
European, 4, 55, 147, 183
evaporation, 33, 109, 111
evaporite deposits, 111-113
Eve, 42, 60-63, 66, 67, 75-78, 82, 84, 192
evolution, 3, 14, 15, 20, 28, 41-43, 50, 51, 75, 79, 81, 96-99, 101-104, 106-109, 161, 191
evolutionists, 2, 14, 15, 23, 24, 40-43, 46, 48, 50, 51, 68, 81, 98, 99, 101-104, 107
faith, 3, 11
Fall, 11, 12, 22, 23, 25, 32, 75, 77-79, 81-83, 107, 144, 145, 158
Fars, 92
Farther India, 54, 57, 85, 86, 165-168
Fellahs, 184
Fertile Crescent, 90, 149, 152
fifth day, 37, 197
Finns, 88
firmament, 33, 158, 159, 195
first day, 31, 33, 36
fish, 37
flat earth, 69, 196
Flood, 2, 3, 11-14, 20, 23, 24, 35, 48, 58, 63, 78, 83, 85, 87, 93-97, 99-137, 144, 147, 154-160, 162, 169, 171, 175, 177, 186, 187, 196
flood stories, 122-124
fog, 107, 157
fossil bearing sedimentary rock, 20
fossil record, 11, 20, 67, 114

fossils, 11, 20, 104, 105, 177
fourth commandment, 38
fox, 102
Framework Theory, 24, 25
France, 56, 91, 139, 140, 150, 168
Freemasonry, 146
Furfooz-Grenelle people, 89, 168
Galileo, 10
Garden of Eden, 38, 59, 60, 75, 76, 115, 161
Gath, 185
Gaul, 91, 168
Gaunt, Bonnie, 38
Gaza, 185
generation, 97
genes, 40, 47, 48, 97, 98
genetics, 43, 46, 48, 49, 97, 99
genocide, 141, 146
Gentiles, 140
geocentric, 9, 10, 69, 193, 194, 196
geocentric solar system, 10
geocentric universe, 69, 193, 194, 196
geography, 73, 115, 116, 122
geological record, 25, 110
geology, 9, 20, 25, 94, 109, 114-116, 126, 131
Georgia, 140
Georgians, 139, 140
Germans, 139
Germany, 91, 168
Getae, 88, 140
Geté, 88
Gibraltar, 56
Gihon River, 73, 74
Gilgamesh, 146
Girgashites, 143
global flood (see universal flood), 105-108, 110-113, 128, 158
Gobi Desert, 85-87
God, 5-8, 11, 12, 16-25, 27-34, 36-39, 41, 45, 48, 51-55, 57-61, 63, 65-71, 76, 77, 79, 81-84, 86, 87, 97, 100, 102-104, 108, 109, 115, 124, 126-128, 131-135, 141, 146, 152, 153, 158, 159, 161-163, 187, 188, 190, 195, 197
Goddess of Equality, 51
Goliath, 185
Gomer, 139
Gomorrah, 62, 154
Goshen, 142
Goths, 88
grapes, 106, 108
Great Britain, 91, 139, 168
Great Pyramid, 116-118, 122, 170, 183
Greater Davidic Catastrophe, 154

Greece, 92, 138, 140, 169
Greek, 65, 169
greenhouse effect, 157, 177
Grimaldi race, 55, 166
Gutians, 90
halite, 111
Halys River, 150
Ham, 141, 143, 144, 147, 183
Hamathites, 143
Hamites, 56, 57, 92, 138, 141, 167, 168, 182, 183
Haran (son of Terah), 153
Haran (the city), 152, 153
Hatti, 150
Havilah, 73, 74, 115, 141
Hebrews, 20, 27, 29, 31, 32, 145, 151, 152, 183
Hebron, 185
heliocentric, 9, 10
Hellespont, 150
Herat, 89
herbivores, 79-81, 105
heresy, 11, 12
Hethites, 143
Himalayan Mountains, 72, 115, 157, 177
Hindu Cush, 73, 74
Hittites, 92, 143, 147, 149-151, 170
Hivites, 143, 186
Horim, 185, 186
Horites, 185, 186
horse, 102
Hungary, 139
Hurrians, 90, 151, 186

Hwang River, 57, 167, 169
hybrids, 44, 45, 47, 134
hyena, 102
Hyksos, 90, 151
Iberia, 150
Iberian Peninsula, 91
Iberians, 91, 140
Idaho, 114
igneous petrology, 114
igneous rock, 114
image of God (see likeness of God), 63, 69, 134, 135, 197
immortal, 69, 79, 80, 82
India, 4, 52-55, 57, 73, 85-87, 93, 165-170, 182
Indonesia (see East Indies), 54, 55, 167, 169, 171, 182
Indo-Afghans, 182
Indo-Gangetic Plain, 53, 54
Indo-Iranians, 56, 182
Indus River, 73, 74, 166, 170
insectivores, 79
insects, 36, 37, 79
inspiration, 8
Ionians, 140
Irad, 86
Iran (see Persia), 53-56, 92, 93, 138, 140, 147, 149, 151
Iranian Plateau, 52, 55, 89, 90, 92, 168
Iranians, 56, 92, 123, 139, 140, 182
Irrawaddy River, 57

Irtysh River, 88, 148
Isaiahic catastrophe, 154
Isle of Rhodes, 140
Isles of the Gentiles, 140
Israel, 62, 162, 190
Israelites, 62, 123, 124, 128, 140, 183, 185-188
Italy, 91, 140, 151, 168
Jabal, 121
jackal, 44, 102
Japheth, 139, 143, 147
Japhethites, 138, 139
Javan, 139, 140
Jaxartes River, 74
Jebusites, 143
Jehovah, 17, 19, 27, 39, 71, 77, 81, 146, 190
Jesus, 21, 64, 71, 76, 83, 125, 126, 132, 161
Jew, 65
Joel-Amos catastrophe, 154
Joktan, 145
Jordan, 186, 188
Josephus, 172
Jubal, 87, 121
Judah, 64, 67, 185
Jurassic period, 175
Kabyle, 91
kangaroos, 103
Karun River, 73
Kashgar River, 74
Kassites, 90, 150-152
Kazan, 86
keep, 60
Kerkha River, 73
Khara-khota, 85
Khazars, 139, 140
Khoisans, 4, 46, 51-53, 69, 100, 165, 182
Khufu, 170, 183
kind, 101, 102
Kirgiz Steppe, 86
Kiriathaim, 186
Kittim, 140
Kizilirmak, 150
Kumar River, 74
lacustrine deposits, 112, 113
Lake Balkhash, 88, 148, 149, 168
Lamarck, J. B., 47
Laplace, P. S., 32
Laufen interglacial period, 52, 165
laws of God, 190
laws of nature, 8, 21-24, 34, 115, 126, 190
Lehabim, 142
Leleges, 90, 150, 151
length of days, 9
lesbians, 192
Lesgians, 139
liberal theologians, 2, 15, 20, 72
Libya, 89, 142, 143
Libyans, 89, 91, 142
life, 37
light, 10, 31, 32, 36
lightening rods, 12
Ligurians, 91, 168
likeness of God (see image of God), 5, 59
Lilith, 192
literature, 9, 123, 155

Lithuanians, 139
local flood, 14, 96, 101, 103, 104, 106, 108, 109, 115, 116, 122, 124-126, 130
Long Day of Joshua, 154
Lop Nor, 86, 178
Lot, 125, 128, 153
Lower Egypt, 90-92, 148, 168, 169, 183, 184
Lower Mesopotamia, 55, 90, 92, 147, 168, 169
Lubim, 142
Lud, 144, 145
Ludim, 142
Lullubians, 90
Luther, Martin, 10
Luwians, 150
Lycaonia, 150
Lydians, 142, 145
Macedonia, 140
Mackenzie River, 57
Madai, 139, 140
Magdalenian culture, 56, 167
Maghreb, 91, 143, 147, 182
Maglemosean culture, 89
magma intrusions, 114
Magog, 139
Malay Peninsula, 54
Malaya, 55
Malays, 182
mammals, 37, 38
mammoths, 104, 105
manna, 124

Marduk, 86, 146
marine life, 105, 106
Mars, 120, 121, 154, 155
marsupials, 103, 104, 106
Massagetae, 88
matter, 11, 17-19, 30, 32, 36, 37, 46, 80, 113
mature creationists, 21
Medes, 140
Mediterranean race, 89-92, 148, 150, 151, 182, 183
Mediterranean Sea, 56, 57, 90, 91, 138, 142, 143, 150, 151
megalithic monuments, 118
Melanesians, 55, 182
Melanides, 86, 87
Melanochroi, 4, 51-57, 69, 89, 90, 92, 93, 102, 134, 141, 147, 148, 151, 165, 167, 168, 180, 182, 183
Memphis, 142
Menes, 142, 148, 169
Mercury, 155-157
Merodach, 86, 146
Meshech, 139, 141
Mesopotamia, 53, 55, 56, 72, 73, 90, 92, 93, 117, 122, 137, 138, 145, 147-149, 151, 152, 168-170
Middle East, 4, 71, 90, 92,

93, 95, 103, 117, 123, 130, 137, 138, 147, 168, 169
military state, 146
Mingrelians, 139
Mins, 182
miscegenation, 1, 41, 45, 62, 63, 97, 128, 133-135, 188
Mizraim, 141, 142, 148, 183
Moab, 62
Moabites, 186, 188
Mongolia, 57
monogenesis, 41-43
monogenetic theory, 42, 43, 50
monogenists, 40
Moon, 27, 33, 35, 36, 108, 152, 175, 176, 190, 195
morality, 7
Moravia, 56
Morocco, 142
Morris, Henry, 14, 20, 24, 103, 116, 174
Moschi, 141
Moses, 33, 72, 100, 124, 187
Mousterian culture, 53
Mu, 85, 123, 131
Mullins, Eustace, 146
Muscovites, 149
mutations, 98, 99
Mysia, 139
Naachals, 86

Naamah, 146
Nafud, 56
Nanna, 152
Naphtuhim, 142
natural laws, 8
natural processes, 21-23, 127
natural selection, 47, 48, 68, 98
nature, 5, 6, 8, 9, 11, 15, 21-24, 34, 38, 44, 45, 49, 51, 68-70, 76, 79, 80, 115, 126, 127, 135, 186, 190
Nazarites, 66
Neanderthals, 53
Near East, 25, 130
nebula theory, 32
Negeb, 185
Negrillos, 182
Negritos, 54, 182
Negroes, 37, 40, 41, 45-48, 51-55, 69, 97-99, 102, 138, 165, 167-169, 180, 182
Neolithic Age, 84, 87, 180
Neolithic culture, 58, 84, 87, 90, 91, 124, 168, 181
Neo-Celts, 149
Nephilim, 100, 134, 146, 185-188
New Guinea, 54, 166, 168
Nile River, 53, 73, 92
Nilotes, 182
Nilo-Hamites, 182

Nimrod, 138, 141, 142, 145, 146, 170
Nineveh, 144, 145
Ninurta, 146
Nippur, 92
Noah, 1-3, 15, 35, 40, 46, 58, 83, 87, 95-98, 100-102, 106-109, 116-120, 122-125, 127, 128, 130-138, 143, 144, 161, 162, 169, 185, 196
Nod, 60, 84, 87, 95, 162, 167
non-Adamic man (see pre-Adamic Man), 37, 82, 137, 198
non-Adamic woman, 143, 144
Noorbergen, Rene, 118, 119, 121, 174
Nordics, 88, 89, 149, 182
North Africa, 56, 91, 117, 138, 143, 166, 167
North America, 57, 167-169, 182
North Sea, 89, 168
Northern Hamites, 182
Nubia, 141, 142
nuclear war, 118
occult, 146
Oceania, 182
Og, 188
one blood, 64

open sewers, 12
opossums, 103
Orientals, 182
origin of races, 98
origin of the Universe, 17
Orion, 146
Ossetes, 140
Oxus River, 74, 137
Pacific Ocean, 85, 131, 156, 177
Padan-Aram, 151, 171
Pakistan, 53, 182
Palaicians, 150
Paleolithic Age, 166, 180
Paleolithic culture, 84, 124
Paleosiberians, 182
Paleozoic Era, 38, 175, 176
Paleo-Celts, 89, 149
Palestine, 90, 138, 142-144, 150, 151, 153, 169, 185-188
Palestinians, 90
Pamir Plateau, 58, 74, 83, 87, 161
Pamiri, 182
Pamirs, 88, 89, 149, 178
Paraoeans, 182
Pathros, 142, 184
Pathrusim, 142, 183, 184
Paul, 76
Pelasgians, 90, 91, 150, 168
Peleg, 138, 145, 155, 156
Peleg Catastrophe, 156
perfect number, 38
Perizzites, 143
Permian period, 37, 175

Index

Persia (see Iran), 138, 140
Persian Gulf, 122, 144, 147, 148, 152, 169
Persians, 92
Pharusia, 142
Philippines, 55
Philistim, 142
Philistines, 185
Phoenicia, 145
Phoenicians, 50, 143
Phrygia, 139
Phrygians, 139
Phut, 141, 143
physical laws, 22, 30, 115
physics, 10, 115, 126
Pictorial Day Theory, 25
Pison River, 73, 74
planets, 10, 13, 18, 30, 32, 193
plants, 20, 34-36, 79, 80, 85, 107, 108, 159, 180, 191
Poland, 56
polygenesis, 41
polygenesists, 41, 42
polygenetic theory, 41, 43, 50
pre-Adamic man (see non-Adamic man), 58, 59, 75, 87, 133-135
Pre-Dravidians, 53, 167, 182
pre-fossil sedimentary rock, 20
Pre-Sumerians, 88, 90, 92, 93, 150

primeval sea, 31
principle of diffusion, 123
principle of speciation, 68
principle of tradition, 123
Proterozoic Era, 34, 38
pteridophytes, 35
quagga, 102
Raamah, 141
races of men, 1-3, 5, 12, 40-42, 44-49, 51, 59, 64-66, 68-70, 77, 96-101, 124, 161, 196-199
racial prejudice, 41
rain, 21, 33, 105, 107, 126, 129, 156-159, 178, 190
rainbow, 109, 131, 132, 158
rain-evaporation cycle, 33
Rebekah, 66
Red Sea, 128, 192
religion, 8, 17, 68
Rephaim, 185, 186, 188
reptiles, 37, 38
Restitution Theory, 12, 24-26
revelation, 5, 7, 8, 17, 24, 68, 125
Rhone River, 91, 140
Riff, 91
Riphath, 139
Riss-Würm interglacial period, 165
Rocky Mountains, 115
Rodanim, 140
Rumania, 139
Russia, 138, 150

Sabbath, 27, 38, 39
Sabtah, 141
Sahara Desert, 52, 142
Saharan-Hamites, 56, 57, 182
Sakae, 88
Salah, 144, 145
salinity of the oceans, 105
salvation, 7, 133, 136
Salween River, 57
sand dune deserts, 113
sandstone, 110
Sarah, 66, 153
Sarai, 153
Satan, 60, 75, 76, 133, 146, 187
Satanic fall, 25
Satechah, 141
Saxons, 139
Sayan Mountains, 88
Scandinavia, 89, 91, 150
science, 3, 5-8, 10, 12, 15-19, 24, 25, 28, 38, 43, 49-51, 67-69, 80, 97, 101, 116, 190, 194
Scriptures, 1, 5-8, 10-15, 17, 19, 22, 24, 43, 46, 48-51, 59, 61, 67, 71, 80-82, 97, 108, 143, 160, 161, 171, 190, 193
Scythians, 140
sea creatures, 37, 197
Seba, 141
Second Advent, 125
second day, 33, 34, 36
second law of thermodynamics, 23
secular evolution, 14, 20
sedimentary rock, 20, 112, 114, 115, 191
sedimentary strata, 105, 114
Seir, 186
selective breeding, 107
serpent, 75, 76
Seth, 62
seventh day, 22, 27, 38, 39, 126
Shambhala, 85
Shem, 143-147
Shemites, 138, 144, 183
Shillouhs, 142
Shinar, 72, 117, 130, 144, 155
Siberia, 104
Sidonians, 143
Silurian period, 35, 175
sin, 7, 12, 40, 41, 45, 62, 63, 69-71, 76-80, 82, 97, 133-136, 162, 188
Sin, moon-god, 152
Sinicus, 182
Sinites, 143
six days of creation, 21, 22, 24-27, 30, 38
sixth day, 28, 34, 37, 38
Six-Day Creation Theory, 12, 20, 24
six-day creationists, 20-23, 78-81

Slavic Prussians, 139
Slavs, 139, 149, 170
sloths, 102
Smith, Joe Pye, 25
Sodom, 62, 126, 154
soil, 21, 34, 36, 96, 113, 159, 180
solar system, 9, 10, 32, 193
Solomon, 66, 95
Solutrean culture, 56, 167
sons of God, 133, 134, 187, 188
Sousa, 90
South Africa, 46, 100, 182
South America, 57, 103, 182
Southern Mediterraneans, 91
space, 17-19, 26, 29, 121
Spain, 138, 140
special creation, 48, 50, 104
species, 101, 102
species of men, 5, 15, 43, 50-52, 58, 63, 70, 71, 99, 102, 134, 180, 182
spermatophytes, 35
stars, 10, 13, 18, 30, 31, 35, 36, 108, 190, 193, 195
Stonehenge, 117, 118, 122
Sudanese, 182
Suebi, 88, 170
Suebians, 88
Sulaiman Mountains, 54, 55
Sumer, 137, 148, 152, 169, 170
Sumerian civilization, 92
Sumerians, 88, 90, 92, 93, 123, 148, 150, 151
Sun, 9, 10, 13, 21, 23, 27, 29, 31-33, 35, 36, 47, 82, 86, 131, 155, 190, 193-196
surgical operations, 11
Susiana, 145
sylvite, 111
Syr Darya, 74
Syria, 56, 138, 143, 148, 150-152, 170
Syrians, 145
Szechwan, 57, 166
Tamar, 66
Tarim Basin, 58, 83, 84, 86-88, 100, 121, 129-131, 134, 162, 167, 178, 179
Tarshish, 140
Tarsus, 140
Taurus, 44, 150
technology, 58, 118-122
Terah, 152, 153
thallophytes, 34, 35
theistic evolution, 14, 213
theistic evolutionists, 15, 81
third day, 20, 34, 35
Thracians, 141
Tibareni, 140
Tibet, 58, 86-88, 167
Tibetan Plateau, 52, 57

Tien Shan, 74, 88, 178
Tigris River, 72, 73, 115, 144
time, 28, 29
Tiras, 139, 141
Togarmah, 139
Tomas, Andrew, 123
Tower of Babel, 117, 122, 145, 146, 154, 155
Triassic period, 175
Trojans, 140
troposphere, 21, 33, 157
Tshcudes, 88
Tubal, 139, 140
Tubal-cain, 87
Tungus, 4, 182
Turanians, 40, 41, 46, 48, 51, 52, 57, 58, 62, 69, 84, 86, 88, 97, 102, 121, 134, 138, 148, 149, 162, 165, 166, 171, 180, 182
Turkestan, 58, 83, 84, 86-89, 92, 93, 129, 130, 137, 147, 149, 168, 170, 178, 179
Turkey, 48, 73, 130
Turkmenistan, 86
Turks, 58, 84, 87-89, 93, 182
Turusha, 141
Ugrians, 148, 167, 182
Uighur civilization, 86
Uighur Empire, 85, 86

Ukraine, 56, 89, 170
Unger, Merrill F., 145, 174
unity of man, 2, 43, 44, 46, 47, 50, 51, 63-65
universal flood (see global flood), 2, 3, 13, 14, 20, 94, 96, 101, 102, 104-106, 108, 110, 112-122, 124, 125, 131, 196
universal flood theory, 13, 14, 20, 94, 113, 114
universalists, 14, 23, 95, 98, 99, 101-107, 109, 122-125, 128, 130, 131, 135, 158
Universe, 6-8, 10, 12, 13, 16-19, 21, 23, 24, 28, 30, 33, 37, 39, 69, 162, 193, 194, 196, 197
Unuk, 85
Upper Egypt, 56, 92, 142, 148, 168, 183
Upper Mesopotamia, 145, 148, 149, 169
Ur, 92, 144, 151, 152, 169-171
Venus, 154
volcanoes, 113
Voltaire, F. M. A., 46
Wadjak man, 54
waste and void, 19, 25
Wends, 139

Western Turkestan, 86, 88, 89, 92, 149, 168, 170
Whitcomb and Morris theory, 14
Whitcomb, John C., Jr., 14, 20, 24, 103, 115, 116, 174
White, 1-5, 40, 41, 43, 46, 58, 65-67, 74, 99, 101, 124, 146, 161, 162, 180, 183
white man, 40, 43, 124, 180
wine, 106
writing, 3, 85, 137, 147, 169

Würm I glaciation, 52, 53
Würm II glaciation, 52, 54, 55, 57
Würm III glaciation, 55, 56
Xembala, 85
Yahu, 124
Yangtze River, 57, 166
Yellow River, 57
Yellowstone Park, 113
Yenisey River, 88
Yunnan, 57, 167
Zagros Mountains, 90
Zamzummim, 185, 188
zebra, 102
Zemarites, 143
Zuzim, 185

Scripture Index

1 Chronicles 1:7, 140
1 Corinthians 14:33a, 8
1 Corinthians 15:45, 63, 64
1 Corinthians 15:47, 64
1 Kings 10:24, 95
1 Peter 3:20, 101
1 Samuel 2:8, 194
1 Samuel 16:12, 66
2 Corinthians 11:3, 76
2 Peter 2:4, 133
2 Peter 2:5, 101
2 Peter 3:5, 6, 131
2 Peter 3:8, 28
2 Samuel 13:1, 66
Acts 2:20, 29

Acts 13:17, 59
Acts 17:26, 63, 64
Colossians 3:11, 63, 65
Deuteronomy 1:28, 185
Deuteronomy 2:10, 186
Deuteronomy 2:11, 185, 186, 188
Deuteronomy 2:20, 188
Deuteronomy 2:21, 185
Deuteronomy 2:22, 186
Deuteronomy 2:23, 185
Deuteronomy 3:11, 188
Deuteronomy 3:12, 188
Deuteronomy 9:2, 185
Ecclesiastes 1:4, 5, 193

Ecclesiastes 3:1, 8
Exodus 9:19-22, 94
Exodus 9:6, 94
Exodus 20:11, 81
Ezekiel 27:14, 139
Ezekiel 28:12-19, 76
Ezekiel 38:6, 139
Galatians 3:28, 63, 65
Genesis 1:1, 12, 13, 16, 17, 25, 26, 30, 31, 36, 158
Genesis 1:2, 18, 25, 26, 31
Genesis 1:3, 26
Genesis 1:3-5, 31, 36
Genesis 1:5, 27
Genesis 1:6,7, 33
Genesis 1:8, 27
Genesis 1:9, 34, 35
Genesis 1:10, 35
Genesis 1:11, 35
Genesis 1:12, 34, 35
Genesis 1:13, 27
Genesis 1:14, 27, 33, 35
Genesis 1:14-16, 33
Genesis 1:16, 27, 108
Genesis 1:20-22, 37
Genesis 1:24-28, 37
Genesis 1:26, 58, 59
Genesis 1:27, 58, 59
Genesis 1:30, 79, 80, 82
Genesis 2:4, 26
Genesis 2:6, 158, 159
Genesis 2:7, 71
Genesis 2:8, 71, 72, 115
Genesis 2:8-14, 115
Genesis 2:10-14, 71
Genesis 2:14, 73
Genesis 2:17, 81

Genesis 2:24, 198
Genesis 3:1, 75
Genesis 3:8, 77
Genesis 3:13, 75
Genesis 3:15, 76
Genesis 3:20, 63, 78
Genesis 3:21, 82
Genesis 3:24, 83
Genesis 4:4, 82
Genesis 4:12a, 84
Genesis 4:14, 61, 95, 96
Genesis 4:15, 61
Genesis 4:17, 61, 63, 85, 87, 121
Genesis 4:17-24, 121
Genesis 4:20, 121
Genesis 4:21, 87, 121
Genesis 4:22, 87
Genesis 5:1,2, 6
Genesis 6:4, 100, 134, 186, 187
Genesis 6:9, 97, 133
Genesis 7:11, 195
Genesis 7:19, 94, 95
Genesis 7:19-24, 94
Genesis 8:1, 109
Genesis 8:2, 195
Genesis 8:22, 8, 106, 190
Genesis 9:3, 82, 83
Genesis 9:9, 10, 109
Genesis 9:20-27, 143
Genesis 10:4, 140
Genesis 10:10, 72
Genesis 10:26-29, 145
Genesis 10:32, 121
Genesis 11:2, 72
Genesis 11:31, 152
Genesis 12:11, 66

Index

Genesis 12:14, 66
Genesis 14:1, 72
Genesis 14:5, 186, 188
Genesis 14:6, 186
Genesis 15:20, 188
Genesis 24:10, 72
Genesis 26:7, 66
Genesis 36:20, 186
Genesis 36:21, 186
Genesis 36:29, 186
Genesis 41:57, 94
Hebrews 11:3, 17
Isaiah 2:9, 198
Isaiah 5:15, 198
Isaiah 11:6-9, 78, 79
Isaiah 14:12-14, 76
Isaiah 31:8, 198
Isaiah 34:14, 192
Isaiah 43:10-12, 161
Isaiah 45:18, 19
Jeremiah 5:22, 190
Jeremiah 5:24, 190
Jeremiah 33:20, 190
Jeremiah 51:27, 139
Job 1:6, 133
Job 9:6, 194
Job 26:11, 195
Job 28:26, 190
Joel 3:18, 29
John 16:23, 29
Joshua 11:21, 185
Joshua 11:22, 185
Joshua 12:4, 188
Joshua 13:12, 188
Joshua 13:3, 185
Joshua 14:12, 185
Joshua 14:15, 185
Joshua 15:14, 185
Joshua 17:15, 188
Joshua 18:23, 185
Jude 5-11, 62
Jude 7, 62
Jude 11, 62
Judges 1:20, 185
Luke 2:1, 94
Luke 17:26-30, 125
Luke 24:42-43, 83
Matthew 23:33, 76
Matthew 24:37-39, 125
Numbers 13:22, 185
Numbers 13:28, 185
Numbers 13:33, 100, 185-187
Proverbs 8:29, 190
Psalm 19:4, 195
Psalm 19:6, 195
Psalm 24:2, 193, 195
Psalm 49:2, 198
Psalm 62:9, 198
Psalm 104:2, 3, 194
Psalm 104:5, 193, 195
Psalm 104:6-9, 158
Psalm 104:21, 82
Psalm 136:6, 193
Psalm 148:4, 159, 195
Psalm 148:5,6, 160
Romans 5:12, 78, 82
Romans 5:12-21, 78
Romans 5:14, 64
Romans 10:12, 63, 65
Songs of Solomon 5:10, 66